Roger A. Philips

Guide to Software Export
A Handbook for International Software Sales

*Pre-publication
REVIEWS,
COMMENTARIES,
EVALUATIONS . . .*

"**T**he *Guide to Software Export* is an excellent, concise handbook for those who are novices, and provides a wealth of information for those who are already in the field. Roger Philips understands that not every company is ready to go international, even as an exporter. His cautions are well-taken, and his advice is sound. He proceeds step-by-step through the processes that an exporter must take, explaining as he goes how one targets country markets, designs an entry strategy, and manages the chosen channel. Philips concludes by presenting a sample distribution agreement, international travel tips, and a collection of well-chosen Internet sites.

I would highly recommend this book to anyone who is thinking about exporting, who has begun to export but still is unsure of the path to follow, and for those who are already in the field. There are gems here, and those with greater sophistication will still come away with satisfaction."

Shoshana B. Tancer, PhD
*Professor, International Studies;
Director, NAFTA Center,
Thunderbird/The American
Graduate School of International
Management, Phoenix, AZ*

More pre-publication
REVIEWS, COMMENTARIES, EVALUATIONS . . .

"**R**oger Philips has achieved the elusive ideal of brevity with detail in his excellent *Guide to Software Export*. This totally practical work speaks pure sense from beginning to end; it is clearly a distillation of broad experience, and has not one trace of the pneumatic qualities of the theoretical management school.

Philips writes in a crisp, accessible style. He has a commanding familiarity with all aspects of the software business from localization, channel strategy, and practical issues of management through to the exotic pitfalls of transfer-pricing and the Foreign Corrupt Practices Act.

Packed with helpful 'how-to's' and 'who-to's,' checklists, and examples, this is the book for real people with real jobs to do. It is also an effective map of the minefields. Anyone about to embark on an international agenda who leaves this book at the bookstore must positively want to fail.

This handbook addresses the attention of the executive/entre-preneur thinking of moving out of his/her home market (or wondering why initial attempts have failed). Philips has described the dynamics of a software business from a natural, holistic standpoint. Any employee of a software house who reads this will see how and why the pieces fit together. This book has serious barrier-breaking potential for the fortunate reader and his or her organization.

Listen well to the warnings. A mistake in entering a new territory not only takes time, money, and precious management resources to correct, but the lost opportunity is gone forever and the damage to your reputation can close a market to you for years. This is the one thing to get right. Using this handbook is a big first step in the right direction."

Lindsay Smith, FCA
Managing Director,
European IT Solutions Ltd.,
Bedford, England

The International Business Press
An Imprint of The Haworth Press, Inc.

Guide to Software Export
A Handbook for International Software Sales

INTERNATIONAL BUSINESS PRESS
Erdener Kaynak, PhD
Executive Editor

New, Recent, and Forthcoming Titles:

Guide to Software Export
A Handbook for International Software Sales

Roger A. Philips

The International Business Press
An Imprint of The Haworth Press, Inc.
New York • London

Published by

The International Business Press, an imprint of The Haworth Press, Inc., 10 Alice Street, Binghamton, NY 13904-1580

Cover design by Marylouise E. Doyle.

Library of Congress Cataloging-in-Publication Data

Philips, Roger A.
    Guide to software export : a handbook for international software sales / Roger A. Philips.
        p.   cm.
    Includes bibliographical references and index.
    ISBN 0-7890-0143-8 (alk. paper)
    1. Computer software—Marketing. 2. Export marketing. I. Title.
HD9696.C62P5 1997
005.3'068'8—dc21
                                               97-14967
                                                 CIP

CONTENTS

ABOUT THE AUTHOR

Roger A. Philips is Vice President, International, for Landmark Systems Corporation, a company that develops and markets proprietary software products worldwide, headquartered in Vienna, Virginia. As the former General Manager, International, for Viasoft, Inc., he was responsible for the company's earning the President of the United States' "E" Award for export excellence. The author of numerous articles that have appeared in *Software Magazine, Computerworld,* and the *System Development Journal,* he is the co-author of the book *Developing the World Class Information Systems Organization.* A frequent international speaker, Mr. Philips has addressed information systems audiences throughout Europe and North America. He is a past Chairman of the Arizona Chapter of the Society for Information Management and serves on the Northern Arizona University College of Business Advisory Council for Computer Information Systems. He is a member of the Association for Corporate Growth and the International Trade Association of Northern Virginia. He welcomes reader correspondence and can be reached at: rphilips@usa.net.

Preface

The global computer market is roughly divided as 40 percent to North America, 25 percent to Europe, 20 percent to Japan, and 15 percent to the rest of the world, according to *Worldwide Information Technology Market,* International Data Corporation figures. If your company's software products are suitable for the world market, your sales should eventually approximate this distribution. In fact, for most successful, mature software companies, that is exactly the case.

The typical life cycle of a software product is in the range of two to seven years. If you are late in entering a new market with a product, you foreclose the potential income from part of that life cycle. Worse, you allow competitors to establish an early lock-in of the market, making your eventual entry more difficult. Foreign markets as well as domestic adhere to this description. For that reason, it is imperative that you enter foreign markets as quickly as is possible, consistent with the maturity of the product and the resources you have available.

Scarcely any company would not like to grow its sales. This book is intended for software executives and managers who are not satisfied with their company's international sales performance, or who have not yet begun to seriously exploit the world market. Selling internationally is not especially difficult or arcane, but it does require planning, common sense, some cultural sensitivity, and plenty of patience to succeed. In this book you will find guidelines on setting up, managing, and expanding your international sales channels; pitfalls to avoid; and recommendations regarding choices you will need to make.

The book is oriented to the commercial packaged software markets. Some content, though useful, may not directly address the special markets of custom, military, or embedded software. It is written from the perspective of a U.S. firm. However, most of the principles are valid for firms of any nationality.

While this book is about selling software abroad, there are many books on international marketing in general. You should read some of these to get a more complete picture of the world of export. See for instance, Herman J. Maggiori's *How to Make the World Your Market: The International Sales and Marketing Handbook,* and William Fath's *How to Develop and Manage Successful Distributor Channels in World Markets*. Further information on all sources and references may be found in the Bibliography.

Acknowledgments

Research assistance, patience, and a multitude of vital tasks—Jeanette Philips.

Legal content, vetting, cheerful corrections, and amplifications—Tom McVey, partner in the Washington firm of Williams, Mullen, Christian & Dobbins.

Editing and encouragement—Kent Petzold and Charles Billingsley.

Excellent advice on how to organize a book-writing project—Robert H. (Bob) Johnson.

Help and input throughout—Bill Lofquist, U.S. Department of Commerce.

Chapter 1

Your International Potential

COMPANY OBJECTIVES

Entering a new international market requires investment. This investment will be in time, money, and management attention. The same would be true for entering any new market. If you are not prepared to make these investments, do not enter the new market—you will fail. How fast your company can grow its markets depends on the management and capital resources available.

If your product or products are not selling well in their home market, now is probably not the time to begin exporting. Shake the bugs out of both the product and the sales model at home before attempting to take them abroad. It is harder, because of the difficulties in travel, communication, and culture, to work these things out in a foreign country. Success in the United States usually drives a successful international software marketing campaign. Much of the U.S. computer industry trade press is either read or excerpted abroad. Your reputation will precede you, and foreign users (or at least sharp resellers) will already want your promising products by the time you reach them. You will have a repeatable sales model you know works in at least one country, and can base your international models on it.

There is also a more intangible requirement for success in world markets. Management must be prepared to be flexible, and to take a worldview. The "way we do things" might not be optimal for the new, international company. There will be accounting changes, organizational stresses, new travel policies, and unusual people wandering about the company offices. Strategic decisions, as well as the myriad daily ones, will have to take on a broader context. Yes, this packaging may be fine for the United States, but how will it be received in France? The pricing book makes sense here, but will it really be usable by 100 value-added resellers (VARs) in their various country markets?

How do we lead an organization to think globally? It takes time and persistence. Without full and enthusiastic support from top management, it will not happen.

RESOURCES

Perhaps you decide that the domestic sales manager be given international responsibility as well. International requires a great deal of management time and attention at the outset, and as a result, domestic sales start to fall off. You have stretched management resources too thin and probably have not made a good decision.

If you spend time setting up an international VAR network, but lack the budget to adequately support it, you have not only wasted time, but quite probably also clouded your reputation in the international reseller community.

The first step, then, is identifying what resources are or can be made available to the international marketing process. How much money, over what time period can be allocated? How important is the associated sales growth to the firm at this time, and how fast can you afford to grow? The answers to these questions lie in such factors as the following:

- Cash available
- Cash flow from current operations
- Current management bandwidth
- How fast competitors are grabbing foreign market share
- The probable cost of the marketing investment
- Time to payback

As a rough rule of thumb, if you are not prepared to appoint at least one full-time manager to international sales, then your company is probably not yet prepared to enter those markets.

International operations will add a level of complexity to your company. For the first time, you may have to contend with foreign currencies, foreign laws, time zones half a day away, and non-English speaking customers. If today's management is not securely in control of the operation, then you do not need these distractions now.

International operations will stress all parts of the company. Will worldwide pre- and post-sales technical support continue to be provided by the same organizations that provide them domestically today? Will resources be adequate? The marketing department will be faced with new types of campaigns in different countries' markets. Development may have to get involved in localization and national language support tasks. All these stresses must be planned for and their solutions budgeted if the overall objectives are to be met. In fact, the entire corporate organization may have to change.

If management has not had significant international business experience, or has not traveled or studied extensively outside the country, this might be a danger signal. International experience must be gained or hired if the worldview is to be suffused within the organization.

There is another type of approach that can overcome some of the difficulties set out above. This is the solution of partnering. If your partner organization(s) have the capital, management depth, and international experience that your own firm lacks, and you can arrive at a mutually rewarding business arrangement, an accelerated entry into some or all of the world market can be achieved.

A few years ago, the small software firm, Knowledgeware, struck a deal with a Big 6 international accounting firm (Arthur Young, later Ernst and Young) to distribute and support its products throughout the world. This accounting firm had a presence in every major world market and handled virtually all of the marketing tasks. Knowledgeware stuck to its successful direct North American marketing. The partnership was phenomenally productive. Unfortunately, after a number of years, Knowledgeware canceled its distribution agreement and attempted to directly staff a worldwide sales operation. This led to disaster. Costs shot up and sales stopped as new offices were set up around the world and the newly expatriate American managers struggled to learn their new markets.

This is but one of the many possible partnership models available. They include distribution, joint venture, licensing, and other arrangements, and will be examined in detail in Chapter 2.

MARKET POTENTIAL

The first step in considering international sales is evaluating the export potential of your products. This way you can determine if the investments and disruptions discussed above will be worthwhile. Some products just cannot be reasonably exported. For example, if your product prepares a U.S. individual income tax return, there probably is not enough world market demand to justify your interest. Stay at home and be happy.

Global market potential can be affected by many factors, the most critical of which are intrinsic exportability, distributability, market size, and competition. This chapter addresses characteristics intrinsic to your products. The market-related factors are examined in Chapter 3.

Localization

Adapting a software product to the specific needs of a geographic market is called localization. Lack of localization is probably the most prevalent barrier to entry into foreign markets. Localization is more important for application software products than for system software products. With applications, the end user is less likely to be an information technology professional, and will be much less forgiving of foreignness in language, appearance, and approach.

Let us examine localization issues one-by-one:

Application Discipline

If the application product deals with processes affected by laws, business practices, or local custom, it is likely to need modification for each country market. Accounting standards, professional practices, and industry structure may all differ. One application firm that has been extremely successful in solving this problem is SAP, which basically delivers a "kit" of functional parts to the user, and lets each user assemble a system using tables which matches its own business practice. But if your product deals with insurance, the law, accounting, medicine, education, or virtually any other professional or industry area, it must be examined critically in light of the requirements of each market. Many basic attributes of these industries vary from country to country.

National Language Support (NLS)

Microsoft Word 6.0 (the single-byte version) supports over eighteen different natural languages and dialects, including three dialects of English. There are also versions for languages such as Chinese, Japanese, and Arabic, which require a double byte (discussed below) for each character. If Microsoft thought this extensive adaptation was necessary for success around the world, so might you. Or maybe not. Some system software products have never been translated from American English, yet are used by thousands of companies worldwide. The system programmers who use them are used to dealing with English software, and would just as soon not pay the increased cost that translation would add to the product.

The point is, you have to research the language issue. For consumer products (such as Word), the differences even between dialects of the same language (Canadian versus Continental French, for example) are critical. The British spell it "colour," use petrol in their cars, and ring clients "on" (not "at") their telephone numbers, or visit their offices located "in" (not "on") their streets.

What has to be translated? Perhaps not everything, but here are some candidates:

• User manuals
• Packaging
• Installation instructions

- Help text
- Programmatic messages
- Screen legends
- Reports
- Internal documentation
- Support instructions
- Marketing materials
- Advertising copy
- Readme files

Full national language support (NLS) goes beyond merely translating foreign words using the familiar twenty-six letters of the English alphabet. Many languages use different letters, ümlauts, gràves, ácutes, diphthœngs, çedillas, tildĕs, and sø forth.

Most languages are less compact than English. Screens designed with only English in mind might look cluttered, or not even fit when translated into Spanish, for example, which takes roughly 40 percent more characters to represent the same thought as does English. Not all languages read from left to right. Arabic and Hebrew are bi-directional, with most characters written right to left, but with numbers and imbedded foreign quotes written left to right.

Then there is the world of double byte. The internal architecture of the hardware may come into play when dealing with double-byte characters. If your product parses character strings, or recognizes inputs in the user's own language, you will have to allow for double byte if you wish to be successful in the 25 percent or so of the world market that uses more than 255 characters in its languages. Some hardware, as an example, recognizes special "shift-in" and "shift-out" bytes to delimit double-byte text. In Japanese, double- and single-byte characters may appear together in the same sentence, delimited by shift-in and shift-out characters.

Not all manufacturers and operating systems use the same kind of double byte character set (DBCS) encoding. The Microsoft standard is called "Shift-JIS." Many UNIX implementations recognize "EUC." Major manufacturers such as Sun, Hewlett Packard, and IBM have moved toward recognizing both of these standards. Your software may need to be able to recognize and correctly process these combinations.

IBM and other manufacturers offer special courses for developers on how to enable software for national language. Microsoft Press publishes *Developing International Software* by Nadine Kano, an excellent handbook for implementing Windows applications for foreign use. Much of Kano's advice is also applicable to non-Windows environments. Such information is mandatory for the inexperienced.

Obviously, it is less expensive and quicker to design NLS into the product from the beginning than to retrofit it. Use such principles as external message files, which can be independently translated. If you use hypertext help, for instance, be sure to choose a hypertext product that is already NLS enabled (some are, some are not). Never hard code literals that might be displayed to users—put them in external tables instead. For example, if your screen displays the literal "press any key," you would like to translate that as part of an external table, which can be done by a nontechnical translator, rather than within the program, which would require a programmer, a recompilation, and a separate version of the source code for each language.

NLS support is not a one-time thing. Once you have enabled a product for a language, it becomes a version, or even better, an integral part of the product that must be updated whenever the base product is enhanced. Documentation changes should be red-lined or marked with sidebars to avoid the expensive task of retranslation at each new release.

Validated technical translation can cost up to U.S. $1 per word. It is best to use translators who are native practitioners in the application discipline of your product. Avoid using less qualified services or students who may lack the knowledge of the exact words used in the appropriate profession or industry. Retranslation back into English can serve to check the accuracy of the original translation. See Table 1.1 for a list of software houses that specialize in NLS adaptation. (Note that for each telephone and fax number in Table 1.1 and throughout this book, a "+" symbol precedes the first digits to denote the country's international access code. Refer to "telephone and fax numbers" in Appendix 6 for more information.)

Table 1.1. Globalizing Your Software

There are a variety of software houses around the world specializing in adapting existing packages to national language support. Among them are:

Johnston & Associates, Inc.
7861 Wilton Crescent
Suite 150
Sarasota, FL 34201

telephone: +1-941-351-8349
fax: +1-941-359-3265
http://www.ja=i18n.com

Log-On Ltd. Software Packages Development
32 Tuval Street
Ramat Gan 52522
ISRAEL

telephone: +972-3-575-11-21
fax: +972-3-752-07-94

MATRIX Corporation
Hakusan-Takayanagi Bldg., 3f
1-7-6 Hakusan
Bunkyo-ku
Tokyo 112
JAPAN

telephone: +81-3-5689-3535
fax: +81-3-5689-3534

MATRIX USA
University Park at MIT
26 Landsdowne Street
Cambridge, MA 02139

telephone: +1-617-527-2776
fax: +1-617-527-2559
email: info@matrixusa.com

SimulTrans, LLC
2606 Bayshore Parkway
Mountain View, CA 94043

telephone: +1-415-969-7600
fax: +1-415-969-9959

SymbioSys, Inc.
15200 Shady Grove Road
Suite 350
Rockville, MD 20850

telephone: +1-301-921-5990
fax: +1-301-527-9060

System 7, Inc.
16133 Ventura Blvd.
Suite 850
Encino, CA 91436

telephone: +1-818-501-0682
fax: +1-818-501-6041

There are NLS considerations beyond language. Conventions differ from the United States on such common items as punctuation, currency, dates, times, and measures.

- *Punctuation.* Most of the world uses a comma, not a period, to separate an integer and its decimal fraction: for example, ten-and-a-half is 10,5. The reverse is true for demarking groups of three zeroes in large numbers: one million is 1.000.000.
- *Currency.* If your product displays dollar signs, it will have to be changed for most markets. Also, the value of foreign currency can make for some very large numbers (U.S. $10 equals a seven-digit number of Turkish lire as of this writing). Thus the storage and display space you have allocated for currency amounts may be inadequate.
- *Dates and Times.* Dates abroad are usually given day/month/year. Foreign users simply will not understand the less logical U.S. convention month/day/year. Times are usually what we think of as military: the twenty-four-hour system.
- *Measures.* Only a few countries have failed to adopt the metric system. Unfortunately, the United States is one of them. All others use meters, grams, hectares, etc. Your products may need modification to accommodate and correctly display metric measures, especially of weight, distance, area, force, temperature, and power.

- *Screen Design.* In addition to the "real estate" problem of sentence and word length in screen and report design mentioned above, your foreign product users may have other cultural sensitivities that would affect the attractiveness of your product. For example, in much of Asia white is the color of death, red connotes happiness, while green is the color for emergencies. An icon representing a typical American mailbox may be meaningless in a country that uses a different shaped "box." Initials on pushbuttons must not be hard coded to stand for their English meanings.

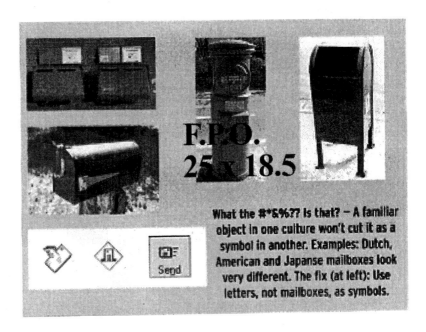

What the #*&%?? is that? — A familiar object in one culture won't cut it as a symbol in another. Examples: Dutch, American and Japanese mailboxes look very different. The fix (at left): Use letters, not mailboxes, as symbols.

Source: Reprinted by permission of *Computerworld*.

- *Sounds.* If your product produces sounds, they may also require localization. Of course, speech may have to be translated. But other stylized sounds, such as the "ta-da" and "raspberry" sounds for success and failure indicators, may not have any cultural relevance to many users and will have to be localized.

- *Rounding.* Surprisingly, the rules for rounding numbers are not universal. In Switzerland and Argentina, for instance, special algorithms are used (said to favor the banks).
- *Sorting.* Sort sequences differ among countries. In Germany, *ä* sorts after *a*. In Sweden, it sorts after *z*. Programming must be sensitive to these nuances to be truly localized.

Hardware and Software Environments

If your product requires certain hardware or software environments to operate, be aware that the fact that such environments are common in the United States may not necessarily indicate that they are also common abroad.

Some hardware manufacturers have been much more successful selling in the United States than elsewhere. There may be different versions or releases of some software products found in different world regions. Even environments that are designated identical by suppliers may, in fact, have subtle differences. Only through testing in the actual foreign environment will these be revealed. In one case it turned out that the "identical" Sun operating system release tended to be linked with a different version of a certain remote procedure call in the United States from that linked in Europe. The vendor's application would not run in Europe, and initially the problem could not even be duplicated in the United States.

In Japan, the operating system MS-DOS is almost entirely replaced by DOS-V, which supports Japanese characters. Sybase has been much more successful in its home market than abroad. Applications packages from SAP are more popular in their home country of Germany than elsewhere. IBM mainframes are largely absent from many formerly communist countries where their export was banned, and from India where imports were banned. The database management system, Adabas, is pervasive in South Africa because, as a European product, it was not subject to the antiapartheid sanctions. IBM mainframes are much more widely used in Brazil than one would expect for the size of the market, because importing smaller computers was banned for many years.

Just because your product is not localized, though, does not mean that the market is closed to it entirely. Some kinds of products do quite well without any localization at all. Many mainframe system products are examples. The users are accustomed to purely English products. Beyond that, there may be a market, though small, for English-only products, even in countries like Japan, which are fairly insistent on local versions. Perhaps you can sell to the foreign multinationals there as a start, to get a toehold in the country, localizing your product in the meantime.

Other Standards

There may be other standards related to the application discipline that require product modification. Many countries and regions have their own standards regarding product quality and performance that may need to be researched. Many European governments, for example, require that all their suppliers, including software suppliers, be ISO 9000 certified. This "quality" standard is difficult and expensive to achieve. See Chapter 3.

For more on exportability, see Joanna Ambrosio's *Computerworld* article, "Should You Export That Software?" (August 2, 1993, p.75).

Export Controls

The sensitive nature of your products in relation to national security may be a factor in their exportability. It may be difficult or impossible to obtain an export license if your products involve cryptography or numerically controlled machining, for instance. See Chapter 3 for further details.

Support Requirements

The support required for your products may in part determine their export practicability. If they are very support intensive, and the support must be rendered in person by highly trained technicians, then obviously export will require more logistical planning and effort. There may be quite cost-effective ways of dealing with this issue, but it must be dealt with if you are to succeed. See Chapter 6 for more details on international product support.

Chapter 2

Global Marketing Approaches

DISTRIBUTION CHANNEL STRATEGIES

. . . if the channel is not established, nothing further can be accomplished.

—Geoffrey A. Moore in *Crossing the Chasm,* p. 168

He who owns the channels owns the market.

There are many choices that must be made in formulating the best distribution channel strategy for each foreign territory, and in choosing those strategies that are best for your company. You will probably be most comfortable with, and be best able to manage, one or perhaps two strategies at any given time. One or two standard approaches (for example, to large and small territories) should be evolved and rolled out as the company is ready.

The choices are discussed in this section. They involve where you will actually have a presence on the ground; how many tiers of representation you will have; whether distribution will be exclusive or nonexclusive; whether you will deal through third parties or your own employees; and, if through third parties, whether they will be agents, distributors, value-added resellers (VARs), master VARs, or original equipment manufacturers (OEMs).

The international distribution strategies you deploy may well differ completely from what you use at home. Markets differ, as do the lengths of supply lines. This may force you to learn new skills and to be creative, but is not any reason not to proceed.

The United States is the world's largest software market. Therefore it is relatively impersonal and anonymous. It is not unusual for salespeople throughout their careers to call on new prospects, meeting potential buyers for the first time, day in, day out, building up relationships from scratch.

Most foreign software markets are not like that. Most experienced salespeople have been in their own small markets for many years. They literally know everybody, and in turn are known by everybody. They have been selling to the same crowd, more or less, their whole careers.

Therefore, an established channel partner who has tested your product and thinks it is good starts you off with two strong advantages—trusting customer relationships, and knowing exactly where to go to sell.

This chapter deals with conventional distribution strategies. See Chapter 5 for electronic distribution options. See also William Fath's *How to Develop and Manage Successful Distributor Channels in World Markets* for a general discussion of indirect international selling.

Local versus Remote

Do you attempt to sell and service your customers locally, in their own country and in their own language; or remotely, from the United States or from another (third) country? Many firms start out with the latter, which represents a low-investment, low-commitment option. Selling internationally from the United States will probably net *some* sales, and can be done with minimal disruption to the corporate structure through the domestic sales organization.

Selling locally requires more time, investment, and management attention. But it is likely to be far more successful in the long run.

Direct versus Indirect

Will your own employees sell and service your foreign customers, or will you engage third parties to undertake these tasks? The former is direct selling, which produces higher gross margins and affords maximum control over marketing activities, but requires much greater investment and management bandwidth.

Most companies start out with indirect selling in new foreign territories until there is a critical mass of customer base to begin direct operations.

One, Two, Three Tiers

How many tiers of distribution should you have? You have probably already answered this question for the domestic market. But there may be a different optimal number for various other world markets.

You will be further away, and with less control over foreign distribution channels. If you are able to directly manage dozens or hundreds of VARs at home, the same may not be true in Brazil, for example. You may need one or more distributors to provide better local support and control.

Advantages

Largely, the advantage of more tiers is more market coverage, by virtue of the multiplier effect. The more tiers you choose, the more entities will be representing your products. There is proportionately less management required on your part as you will be managing only the top tier directly.

Disadvantages

There are also many disadvantages of multitiered distribution:

- Customers usually prefer to deal as closely to the vendor as possible.
- Installation and support of a complex product may simply be impractical for lower tier entities because of the investment in training and specialized staff required.
- Your marketing message will inevitably be diluted as tiers deepen.
- Training, both sales and technical, becomes a bigger task as more entities become involved.
- Most important, more tiers mean a longer "food chain"; more levels of distribution needing a slice of the revenue pie to become motivated to invest in and sell your products.

Unless your products are very high priced or high volume, there may not be enough margin for more than a single, or at most a two-tier, distribution model.

Exclusive versus Nonexclusive

An aggressive partner will naturally want an exclusive agreement. Exclusivity means that you agree not to compete, either directly or through another partner, for sales of the same product in that territory. The exclusive nature of the contract is intended to encourage the distributor to make the investment necessary to strongly market your products. The advantages for the exclusive partner are as follows:

- All marketing efforts made in the territory will eventually accrue to the partner, not to another distributor in the territory.
- There will be no wasted effort in competing against another partner, or against you, the licensor for sales of the product.
- There will be no price competition for the product within the territory.

These are generally advantages for you as well, because channel conflict within a territory is one of the most difficult elements of distribution to manage. The disadvantage for you is that your exclusive partner may not have the market presence and wherewithal to fully cover and penetrate the entire territory. If your exclusive partner fails through either poor performance or lack of investment, to achieve acceptable sales levels, you are then faced with terminating the distribution agreement. With a nonexclusive arrangement, you need merely appoint more distributors and not further concern yourself with the nonperformer.

Often, a reselling organization will have particular strengths in a particular geography within the territory: it will be focused on only certain (but not all) vertical industries wherein your product can be sold; it may not have the language capabilities to effectively sell into parts of the country (in Belgium, for example, you need French speakers to sell effectively in Wallonia); or it will have strength only in certain hardware or system software platform environments. In these cases, you might need to subdivide the territory, or might decide to have multiple nonexclusive channel partners.

Your candidate partner will then probably argue that you should not have to deal with multiple partners in his country, that that is too complicated and detailed a task for you. Your partner is then likely to ask for rights to appoint subdistributors to make up any deficiency in his own distribution coverage. This approach has its own pros and cons, which were discussed above.

Another varation of exclusivity is that you retain the right yourself to sell into the territory. This might be viewed as cherry picking by your partner, and could certainly be demotivating, but could be reserved for cases of multinational customers licensing in multiple territories, for instance.

Note that exclusivity is technically illegal in the European Union (see Chapter 3).

Channel Conflict

Ken Lewis, in *Selling Software in the Global Market, 1996-97,* reported that U.S. software firms found channel conflict in foreign channels to be much less a problem abroad than in North American markets. Whereas 27 percent indicated channel conflict was a major sales channel issue in North America, only 7 percent said that it was a major problem in Western Europe, the foreign geography where it was felt to be the worst. (See Figure 2.1.)

Nevertheless, this issue must be addressed if you appoint multiple partners in any given territory. Otherwise your partners will be reluctant to do any territory-wide marketing whose benefits might accrue to another, competing partner. Also, you risk price-cutting battles in channel conflict which can damage the channel, the market, and you.

Approaches to deal with conflict are the same as those which you might use at home. A prospect registration system might work, wherein a prospect is reserved if it is reported on a monthly sales forecast within the previous ninety days. Teaming is another approach. Be cautious of not violating anticompetitive laws of the European Union with any such plan in Europe. Channel conflict should be a relatively rare occurrence. If it is happening frequently, unless your product is already a household name with a demand-driven market, you may have too many channel partners in the territory, and have reached the point of diminishing returns.

Figure 2.1. International Sales Channel Major Issues

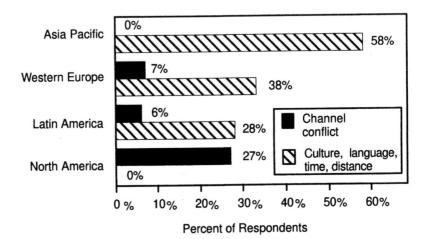

Source: Reprinted by permission of *The Culpepper Letter.* (Alpharetta, GA: Culpepper and Associates, 1996).

Country versus Multicountry versus Intracountry Territories

Should distribution territories correspond with national borders or should they be larger or smaller? These answers depend on the size of the market and the capabilities of the available channel partners. Although it is more costly in terms of support and management time and attention, separate distributors for each country is a less risky and more flexible strategy. Thus the Nordic territory could be handled by one distributor or by four. In a typically large market like Germany, regional differences might argue for, say, four distribution geographies, perhaps centered in Munich, Hamburg, Berlin, and Frankfurt.

Other territory groupings that may make geographical sense to aggregate for distribution are:

- French-speaking: France, the French-speaking Swiss cantons, and Wallonia in Belgium
- Dutch-speaking: the Netherlands, and Flanders in Belgium

- Italian-speaking: Italy, and Canton Ticino in Switzerland
- German-speaking: Germany, Austria, and the German-speaking Swiss cantons
- ASEAN (Association of SouthEast Asian Nations): Brunei, Burma, Indonesia, Malaysia, Singapore, Thailand, the Philippines, and Vietnam
- Benelux: BElgium, the NEtherlands, and LUXembourg
- MERCOSUR (the "southern cone" common market): Argentina, Brazil, Chile, Paraguay, and Uruguay
- Venezuela and Colombia
- The Orient's "double-byte" territory: China, Hong Kong (part of China since 30 June 1997), Japan, Korea, and Taiwan
- Central America and the Caribbean
- Saudi Arabia, Kuwait, Oman, the United Arab Emirates, Qatar, and Bahrain
- Australia and New Zealand
- The United Kingdom and Ireland
- Iberia: Spain and Portugal
- Eastern Europe
- The Commonwealth of Independent States (the former Soviet Union)

Geographical groupings that are unlikely to be successfully grouped under one distribution partner include countries with present-day enmities. One software firm added Moslem Turkey to the territory of its Israeli distributor and wondered why no sales were made there. Similarly, a Turkish firm would be unlikely to succeed in Greece. The point is to sufficiently understand the politics, cultures, and religions of countries to avoid grouping them into illogical territories.

The "Pan-European Distributor"

Unless your market is very thin, be especially wary of appointing a single distribution partner for all of Europe. Very few firms have the ability to adequately cover this large, diverse territory. If you do choose to enter into such an arrangement, be sure you have the ability later to sever various country markets that may not be producing adequate sales.

Telesales

There is a lower limit of transaction price consistent with face-to-face selling. Geoffrey A. Moore, in *Crossing the Chasm,* says this number is about U.S. $50,000. Others put the lower limit at U.S. $15,000. Below the limit, going to the customer to sell directly on her premises is not profitable. Telesales, retail, bundling, and VARs are possible alternate distribution approaches for low-priced products.

In many countries, the culture for buying over the telephone just does not exist. In fact, telesales would be viewed as offensive in a business-to-business context in some countries. In Latin America, Japan, and many European countries, the personal touch when selling is just too important to be done effectively by telephone.

That is not to say that many portions of the sales cycle cannot be handled by telephone. Initial qualifying, appointment making, seminar invitations, and gathering market intelligence all may be achievable by telephone. But satisfy yourself that a viable precedent for actual teleselling of comparable products exists in a new foreign market before making a major investment in this approach.

The above are consequences of the following characteristics of many foreign business cultures:

- Personal relationships are key to selling—people just will not buy from strangers.
- Countries are smaller—people in an industry know each other, and there is less excuse for not showing up in person.
- You must be there—using telesales to sell remotely will raise the fears of the buyer that you will not be there when she needs you.

LOCAL DISTRIBUTION OPTIONS

There are generally five ways to approach software sales in a foreign market: directly; or indirectly through distributors, agents, or OEMs; or electronically. The direct approach promises the highest returns in the long term, but also requires significant up-front investment. It entails setting up a branch or subsidiary and offices in the territory, and hiring nationals to sell and support the product. A customer base and reputation must be built from scratch. This approach is the slowest starter.

Among these five methods are hundreds of variations and combinations that can be used. In Chapter 10 of *Cracking the Global Market*, Jack Nadel describes the pros and cons of various classical distribution models. "There a hundred different ways to distribute . . . Theoretically, the more direct your distribution, the better off you are" (p. 169). But, "There are costs for distribution, and they are borne either by the distributor or the manufacturer" (p. 169). His point is that whoever absorbs these costs must do so profitably.

Indirect Options

"Distributor" and "agent" are legal terms. Local law often protects agents in special ways that might seem peculiar to those familiar only with U.S. law. Simply speaking, a distributor takes possession of your goods, while an agent does not. See Maggiori's *How to Make the World Your Market* for a thorough discussion of making the agent/distributor decision. As Maggiori says, "this decision is a 'biggie'" (p. 99). In the software world, there are various flavors of each, some of which are defined below (and for a more detailed explanation of distributors and agents, as well as a summary of national laws governing these relationships, see William Fath's *How to Develop and Manage Successful Distributor Channels in World Markets*).

"Classical" Distributor

Selling through an established distributor gives a much quicker liftoff to sales in the territory. The distributor sells relatively easily to his existing customer base, with whom he has a reputation. The established distributor has a sales and support force in place, whose cost is shared among several product lines. Typically 40 percent to 70 percent of revenue is kept by the distributor, who pays all up-front costs. The distributor divides his loyalties among different vendors. A distributor may sell either directly to end users or through VARs, or both.

U.S. software companies have a fairly sorry history of using distributors to do the hard and risky work to establish a foreign territory, then pushing the distributor aside to run the territory directly. Foreign distributors know this, and are sometimes wary of establishing new distribution arrangements with U.S. software companies. It will give the distributor more incentive if a mutually profitable exit strategy is defined up front. This will typically occur when territory gross sales reach a certain threshold figure per year. One approach toward alleviating this concern is agreeing up front to establish a joint venture at the threshold point. The new company would be jointly owned, with minority participation by the distributor. Another is a very sweet buyout provision based on a multiple of the previous year's sales in the territory.

Agent

An agent may represent one or more vendors. She is paid commissions (often in the 10 percent to 25 percent range) and expenses, but does not take a salary or become an employee. An agent can commit the company financially, and, in many countries, can be very expensive to terminate. The agent does not "take possession" or sublicence product. You as the vendor enter directly into contracts with the end users, and invoice and collect from them. This approach, a halfway measure, includes many of the disadvantages of both direct and indirect distribution.

VAR

The value-added reseller (VAR) is generally a small business that will take your product and deliver it as part of a specific, discrete, application-specific solution, or will resell it into a niche market which is either vertical or geographic. VAR selling is often two-tiered, with distributors between the developer and the VAR.

Master or Super VAR

This is a VAR that uses other lower-tier VARs. Before you set up this kind of arrangement, be sure that there is enough margin in each tier of the channel to properly cover the duties to be performed by that tier, plus a reasonable profit, without cutting into your own margin. The "food-chain" can get only so long before it breaks.

Retail

If your product sells to consumers, then retail is an option. Because of limited shelf space and thousands of available titles, retail is typically available only to proven, top-selling products. Retail is not the likely way you will enter major new foreign markets. This distribution approach typically follows a two- or three-tiered model.

OEM

With original equipment manufacturer (OEM) sales, a hardware or software manufacturer licenses the software bundled with its own and other products. The entry costs are low, startup is slow, but these relationships can be long-term revenue producers. Be sure that the other distribution agreements you sign in each territory do not foreclose you from entering freely into OEM agreements for the product, which may or may not be private-labeled by the OEM.

System Integrator

This is typically a large company, also called a system house, which integrates your product into its custom solution for the customer. These relationships may take time to cultivate, but will pay off repeatedly if successful.

Outsourcer

Major firms that take on the information systems management function on behalf of their clients also make valuable international customers. They are very selective, but always looking for software products to make their own operations more efficient. Once your product has been made a standard by an outsourcer, it will be bought all over the world by the firm as it wins new customers.

Direct Options

Direct selling requires a significant investment in both time and money. At the point that you decide that direct representation in a foreign territory is right for your firm, you will need to choose the form of legal entity that you will operate from. Each has important liability and tax aspects which must be evaluated carefully before you proceed.

Subsidiary

A subsidiary is a full, legal corporation, which is registered with the national government of the territory to do business there, and is owned wholly or in part by your firm. There may be several forms of incorporation in each jurisdiction, which in turn may depend on the initial capitalization and form of ownership.

A subsidiary (or sub) may hire employees, trade commercially, enter into contracts, and contract debt. One of the major advantages of the sub over other forms of presence, although often ignored, is the limitation of liability against the parent which this corporate form provides.

Branch

A branch will generally have the same trading privileges of a subsidiary, but is a legal extension of its parent company. Operationally, there will likely be no differences between a subsidiary and a branch, though legally and tax-wise the differences may be substantial.

Also, the message you subtly send the marketplace with a branch is one of a bit less permanence and commitment than with a sub.

Representative Office

Some countries, such as the United Kingdom, permit a single employee of your company to act on your behalf in that jurisdiction without the necessity and cost of establishing a legal entity. Registration is still required, but is relatively simple.

Informal

Certain jurisdictions permit limited commercial activity on the part of foreign employees in that country without any registration whatsoever. This may be useful for management or support offices that do not themselves trade. The limitations are strict, and obtaining good local legal advice in advance for any of these options is recommended.

Joint Ventures

Whether initially established as a joint venture (JV) or as a result of a successful distribution arrangement in a territory, the joint venture is a hybrid entity that can yield benefits as well as headaches. A JV is a legal company, owned jointly by two or more parties. Each owner contributes certain assets to the new JV. Examples of startup contributions include cash, loans, real estate, distribution rights, expertise, management services, and intellectual property.

Critical to the success of the venture is the agreement among the owners as to how the JV will be managed, royalty rates and pricing, how the profits are to be shared, minimum performance standards including liquidity and margin levels, and what actions will be taken in the event of certain contingencies. Questions which must be definitely answered in the JV agreement are who sits on the board, how new board members are chosen, how management is chosen and replaced, and what staffing levels are authorized.

Before any JV can be meaningfully contemplated, a business plan must be drawn up which is agreed upon by all parties. Then the JV agreement can be structured within a rational context. The agreement should deal with what each party has to offer, and what each expects to receive from the venture. Most important is the exit strategy. No JV lasts forever. A noncontentious exit strategy spelled out in the agreement will save possible rancor and even legal costs later. Exit strategies may include a buy-sell agreement, an independent valuation for buyout, or a buyout formula based on sales or earnings.

Combinations

Because you have a subsidiary in a country does not preclude you from also having one or more distributors, VARs, or even joint ventures. Depending on the nature of the market and your product(s), more than one channel type may be required to adequately cover the territory.

In large countries such as Germany, for instance, which may lack a single major urban market focus, adequately covering the whole country from one office may be impossible, and multiple channel options necessary, at least in the beginning.

PRICING

Uplift

In many territories you can obtain a higher price for your products than you can in the United States. There is no obligation on your part to have uniform, worldwide pricing, nor is this generally the best strategy. Higher prices in many countries can be justified, if such justification is even necessary, on the basis of expensive infrastructure and small market size. Telephone calls, gasoline, airfares, and taxes in Europe can range from double to four times their equivalent costs in the United States. Economies of scale, such as having a single hot-line support center, are diluted by having to be able to deal in the local languages. These and other factors make doing business abroad generally more expensive than in the United States, and prices can reflect the cost. Remember, approximately half the price of software goes into marketing and sales, and these costs are a function of local infrastructure.

The factor by which your domestic prices are increased for a market is referred to as *uplift*. This is typically anywhere from 5 percent to 50 percent. One common approach in the United Kingdom is for the sterling price to be set numerically equal to the dollar price. As of this writing, this equals an uplift of about 50 percent. The exact amount probably will be set by custom in the territory, and will be dependent on your market position, competition, and maturity of the market. Mature competitive markets tend to settle into commodity pricing, which may reduce or even eliminate uplifts.

Be cautious here. A multinational customer may well demand uniform worldwide pricing. Be sure you get a large volume buying commitment in return for such a concession, and be sure that your channel partners are in the loop on this strategy. Many software firms do not publicize their prices, and so attempt to avoid the inevitable "gray market" country shopping or complaints that could arise from general knowledge of the amount of uplift.

Exchange Rates

When the dollar is weak, your U.S. prices will be relatively more attractive to the foreign buyer. When the dollar is strong, your prices will seem high. You may wish to take some actions to take advantage of these situations, which will be constantly changing, both on a general worldwide basis as well as country by country.

You can raise your dollar prices where the dollar is weak, but may have to lower them where it is strong. The strong dollar generally discourages imports and may make the whole selling process more difficult.

In any event, exchange rates will materially affect your sales forecasts, as well as the perceived cost of doing business in each country.

Entry Pricing

In order to get a rapid liftoff in a new territory, it is not at all unusual to offer a sharply discounted or even zero price to the first customer or two. Especially if they agree to act as a reference site for other prospects and the press, this is often worthwhile.

However, merely giving product away to a marginally interested customer accomplishes nothing. The early prospect must be ready, willing, and able to fully utilize your software.

TAX EFFECTS

Sales or royalty income you receive from abroad is taxed, just as other income is. When you have foreign direct operations, several complications arise. Briefly, foreign subsidiaries are taxed in their jurisdictions on their own profits (or in some jurisdictions, on their "imputed profit" if they are nonrevenue-producing operations such as service centers). The amount sent off to the parent as royalty or discounted license purchase price is a deductible expense in the subsidiary's jurisdiction, and is taxable to the parent. Foreign branches are taxed as an integral part of their parent entity.

All aspects of international tax comprise a very complex and ever-changing discipline. Much depends on the tax treaties in effect between the countries involved. Consultation with your international accounting firm prior to establishing any international business structure is mandatory. The local office of your accountant will liaise with its office in the country of interest in rendering a proper recommendation to you.

You need not stay with a simple, two-tiered structure of subsidiaries and branches. The subs can themselves have subs and branches in various countries, and so on, all structured to minimize taxes to the parent. Usually subordinate as a consideration, but important, is the pass-through of legal liabilities. In general, the parent is directly liable for a branch's activities, but may be shielded by the corporate veil from legal actions against its subsidiary.

The following discussions on transfer pricing and avoiding "trapped" profits and losses are of a general nature, and must be verified with international tax experts in each particular case.

Transfer Pricing

The calculation of pricing between related corporate entities is called *transfer pricing,* and is a science in itself. Obviously, it is a subject that is of interest to the taxing authorities, as it can help shift income from high-tax-rate jurisdictions to lower ones. In general, if you treat related and unrelated companies alike in this manner, you have a justifiable position. But more aggressive approaches can also survive government scrutiny.

Billing the high-tax-rate sub for management services from the parent, for example, can be a useful approach. The United States is more aggressive than most other countries in investigating and enforcing transfer pricing regulations, so structuring transfers to increase your U.S. tax is more likely a safe position than vice versa.

Avoiding "Trapped" Profits and Losses

If in a given tax year your domestic operation is profitable and your sub is not, you would like to offset the loss against the profit and minimize your domestic income tax. Conversely, if the parent makes a loss and the sub is profitable, you would like to reduce or eliminate the subsidiary's foreign tax liability by using the parent's loss.

The forecast of the relative earnings of the parent and sub is one of the major factors in deciding on the appropriate multinational corporate structure. Using the principles of consolidation under tax law, and with the help of experts, this can often be accomplished.

FINANCING SOURCES

There are a variety of special financing sources that become available to you specifically because you are involved in international commerce.

Domestic Sources

EXIMBANK (Export-Import Bank of the United States)

The U.S. government offers, through local banks, a program of loan insurance aimed at promoting exports. The idea is that you as the exporter arrange a loan through a bank with your foreign receivables as collateral. This increases your working capital, and permits you to accelerate your export program. Normally most bankers would not touch such a loan with a long pole. But with the risk insurance, the government steps in should there be a default. Still, most banks do not write this kind of business. Locate those that do through EXIMBANK. (See Chapter 3, Internet sources.)

OPIC (Overseas Private Investment Corporation)

OPIC promotes economic growth in developing countries and emerging markets by encouraging U.S. private investment through the following programs:

- Financing investments through direct loans and loan guarantees
- Insuring investments against political risk
- Providing investor services such as the Opportunity Bank, a matchmaking service, an information clearinghouse, and investment missions

- Supporting privately-owned and -managed equity investment funds, such as the Israel Growth Fund which invests in business opportunities in Israel

OPIC might help you finance setting up an owned operation in a developing country. Contact them at the following:

OPIC
1100 New York Avenue, NW
Washington, DC 20527

telephone: +1-202-336-8400
fax: +1-202-408-9859

OPIC Information Line
telephone: +1-202-336-8799

Local Sources

National/Local Governments

Many national, regional, and municipal entities abroad aggressively promote foreign investment in their territories. If you have any thoughts of setting up your own operations abroad, it is well worthwhile to contact the appropriate agencies. Because of overlapping territory responsibility, you may be best served to deal with several at once.

These agencies, many of whom have offices in the United States, will host your site visits; wine and dine you; and, more important, offer tax and sometimes cash incentives if you plant an office and hire locals in that territory.

To find these agencies, contact the country's local embassy or consulate.

Venture Capital

Although not as abundant as in the United States, venture capital is available abroad. Sometimes a foreign venture firm may be interested in investing in your company, especially if you have or establish a presence in their home country.

Your foreign bank may help identify such sources and introduce you.

SERVICES

From your experience in selling your products domestically, you will know whether services form a necessary part of your "whole product" offering. If they do, then you will certainly need to make those same services available in your foreign markets. Over any length of time, those services must be supplied locally to be cost efficient, though in startup mode they can come from the domestic services organization.

Although services may not be required to support your products, they may represent an attractive source of additional revenue for the international channel. They may include training, implementation, and usage, and may be of a short duration or become very long term.

Offering the "Whole Product"

The concept of the "whole product" is put forward in Theodore Levitt's *The Marketing Imagination*. Roughly speaking, the whole product is that combination of the delivered product, plus ancillary products and services that may be necessary to use the delivered product fully. These ancillary offerings may or may not be supplied by the original product vendor, but unless and until they are supplied by someone in the marketplace, the delivered product user is placed in "inventor" status, and the product cannot be considered mainstream.

In software, the delivered product is what comes in the package or on the magnetic media. Adding services to the product, books, or "aftermarket" add-ons from different vendors helps users use your product and adds value to the initial sale.

See also *Crossing the Chasm* by Geoffrey A. Moore on the topic of offering the "whole product."

Bundled or Add-On

Do you bundle services into the product sale, or are they priced separately? While bundling may work fine in a directly-served market, it can open up a problem area when the services are performed by third-party channel partners. You have to make sure that your royalties are based on the fair value of the product. This is easy in a list price sale, but if the partner has to discount, how much of that discount applies to your product and how much to the partner's services? Similarly, if you normally enjoy an uplift in the territory, that uplift should not all be allocated to the services. Be sure that the answers to these questions are agreed by both parties in writing before prices are communicated to prospects.

Implementation

You will find it very difficult to provide services in a foreign market without having those individuals who are to render the services as residents in or very near to that market. Thus, if you lack a direct presence in a region, you will most likely look to your sales channel partners to be the providers of training and implementation services for your product.

Do not expect to profit directly from services rendered by your channel partners. Very few successful models exist in the software business for "franchised" services, where you get a royalty for services rendered by third parties using, for example, your training manuals. Such arrangements would be difficult to enforce and would likely be ambiguous, as the shape in which a service is delivered is infinitely variable, as opposed to a product which is well-defined.

It is better to view the profit on services rendered by your channel partners as added margin for them, and additional incentive for them to sell the products in the first place.

Revenue Implications

Priced services, if performed by your own staff, add revenue. This kind of revenue, whether it be from post-sale implementation consulting, training, or long-term advisory work, can serve both to smooth out the revenue cycles characteristic of the pure product selling operation and add to the bottom line. Yet services are typically not as high-margin as product sales.

Consider these options when crafting your international business plan.

Chapter 3

Selecting Target Country Markets

Having critically examined your candidate product for export-ability, and having determined that it will be exportable to at least some countries with an acceptable amount of adaptation, your next step is to determine the potential of the various world markets. From this, you can prioritize your market entries and estimate projected sales volumes. This information, in turn, will be used to construct the business plan you will need to justify and guide your company's export effort.

Each country market, or group of closely related countries, should be evaluated in terms of market size for your product, type, and intensity of competition likely to be encountered, and the availability of viable distribution options there.

Doing business abroad is in some ways easier than it has ever been. The U.S. government, recognizing the country's serious balance of trade deficits, actively encourages all types of export. Trade barriers are falling worldwide. International communication has improved, with the Internet and fax having become instantaneous, inexpensive *de facto* standards.

Nevertheless, each country has its own unique laws, culture, and customs. These must be understood and incorporated into any successful business venture there.

POTENTIAL OPPORTUNITIES
AND BARRIERS TO ENTRY

Competition

It is important to evaluate your competition in each potential market. If a market is fully penetrated, unless you have a clearly superior product it may not pay to attempt to enter it. On the other hand, if competition is flourishing in a less-than-penetrated market, this may indicate the potential for success. Your competitors will very likely be doing well in some markets and poorly in others. This is often due to the varying effectiveness of their sales channels in those markets. Where they are doing poorly, you may do well if you choose your channel strategy carefully. Conversely, their poor performance may indicate that there just is not a good market for either their products or yours in that country. You will need to determine why a competitor is not succeeding before plotting your own strategy.

There have been instances where a competitor was alone in a small country market, and was doing very well by merely order-taking. When a second competitor entered the country with active marketing and sales, the new player garnered superior market share before the first player discovered what was happening and was able to effectively react.

Similarly, a single-competitor market will very likely support high pricing. As a new competitor, you can come into the market with lower, though still adequate, pricing and garner market share quickly. In a highly penetrated, very competitive replacement market on the other hand, prevalent pricing may be too low to justify any investment on your part. In that case, you are simply too late for that market.

The form of distribution your competitors have established may also be instructive. If they either are not present or are all using only indirect distribution, this probably indicates a market which is either small or relatively new. One or more competitors with direct presence indicates a large or more mature market. Unless the market is already fully penetrated, this situation would indicate an opportunity for you, albeit one that might require some significant investment.

The presence of established competition in a foreign market can be a very positive sign. It means that you will not be there first to try to educate the marketplace on the need for the product category, usually a long and expensive process. Active competition means active sales cycles. It is usually easier to get included for consideration in an active sales cycle than to start a sales cycle. This situation also indicates the presence in the country of knowledgeable people who are already familiar with your market niche. If they see the proper incentives, these individuals could help you, as potential employees or partners, onto the fast track for success in that market.

Estimating market penetration and the presence of competition will probably take the form of field work research, as described later in this chapter.

Distribution Environment

The availability of viable distribution alternatives will influence the marketability of your product. Some countries have well-developed distribution channels from which you may choose. Others may lack such alternatives. The best distributors may already represent your competitors. In the mainframe arena, there has been a serious decline in the number of viable distributors in most countries as the market has matured. Because of economic or other factors, the option of your own subsidiary may be less than attractive.

If good VARs or distributors are scarce, it may require a sweeter than normal royalty or discount rate to sign one up. Many country markets involving small and medium size computers are disorganized. In UNIX and Microsoft Windows markets, for instance, rarely will one channel partner adequately cover all platforms, industries, and geographies in the territory. In that case, you are faced with the possible need for identifying, signing, and supporting multiple partners in the territory, and quite possibly, also faced with the channel conflict problem.

ECONOMIC FACTORS

Just as at home, economic factors abroad can be very influential or even overriding to the success and timing of any business venture. There are more varieties of economic conditions, exhibited often to much greater extremes, in certain countries than has been the case in the United States over the past half-century. Knowing and foreseeing these conditions will help in forecasting relative success and appropriate investment levels in each territory. They could also help in determining the relative priority of entry or expansion into new markets.

Economic Climate

Hyperinflation, currency controls, nationalization, privatization, recession, depression, economic boom times—all will affect business in the country experiencing them. In severe recessionary times, for example, most software purchasing decisions are postponed, deferred, delayed. It is not an opportune time to enter a market.

Hyperinflation, on the other hand, may or may not be a show-stopper. While it is antithetical to a sound economy, business may still find a way to get done. In Brazil up until 1993, inflation was measured in percent per day, or hundreds of percent a year. A new currency was decreed every few years so that the number of trailing zeroes could be kept in check.

As a result, most business-to-business transactions were denominated in an inflation-adjusted pseudocurrency. Spare cash was held in "overnight" accounts in banks which kept pace with the inflation rate. Brazilian companies requested that their large customers notify them the day the customer was planning to make a payment. The companies employed runners whose main function was to hurry to the customer, collect the payment, and deposit it in the nearest bank. Waiting for the mails or even ordinary overnight couriers would have reduced the value of payments substantially.

Needless to say, this is no climate for the unwary. In most cases, for a foreign company exporting to Brazil, there was a simple solution—specify payment in U.S. dollars (or Swiss francs or Japanese yen, or some other hard currency). It should be noted that as of this writing, both Brazil and Argentina, two notoriously high-inflation countries in past decades, have both successfully pegged their currencies to the U.S. dollar.

Currency controls can be a more difficult issue. Brazil, several other Latin American countries, and South Africa, among others, have at various times imposed controls on making payments out of the country. During 1995 and part of 1996, Venezuela had currency controls in place. Such controls are generally intended as emergency measures to prop up a critically weak economy. They attempt to keep currency from fleeing the country and to limit the purchase of imports. In effect, the exporter can be paid for goods, but only in that country, and only in local currency. The currency cannot be converted to hard money, and dollars cannot be taken out of the country. What do you do?

Of course, if this is the case before you commence doing business, you might decide to go elsewhere first. There are solutions, none fully satisfactory:

- *Put your money in a local interest-bearing account and wait for controls to be lifted.* Drawbacks: the interest may not keep up with inflation; the currency may be devalued relative to your own; banks may fail; the government (as happened in Brazil several years ago) may freeze all bank accounts for a period of time; you may have to wait a long time for controls to be lifted.
- *Use the money locally—hold a distributor conference or sales quota club in the country; buy airline tickets there, invest in local real estate or the stock market.* Drawbacks: you are allowing an external event to influence your actions and distract you from your main business of selling software.
- *Counter trade—purchase some local export item and try to find a foreign buyer who will pay you in hard currency.* Drawback: you are no longer in the software business when you start this. This is a new business with all associated risks.
- *Stop doing business for the duration.* With foresight, and following a clause similar to 13d(ii) in Appendix 3, you will have the right to terminate your third-party distribution agreements in the country in the event of controls.

Privatization can be excellent for business. In the early 1990s, Mexico privatized its banks. They emerged from being stodgy governmental bureaucracies to become aggressive, competitive companies with a voracious appetite for new technology. Nationalization tends to have the opposite effect.

A sudden devaluation (and they almost always are) can adversely affect you, even if you price in dollars. A sale that is almost completed (or even already completed) may start to unravel when the customer realizes that the price for your product in terms of his own currency has just increased dramatically. Do not be surprised to receive an urgent call for renegotiation in those cases.

Economic Forecast

Times of economic expansion are generally attractive to the export trade. Look at the absolute economic growth rates of all your existing and intended markets. Anything less than zero is a danger signal. One percent or 2 percent growth means a sluggish economy. Three percent to 5 percent is healthy growth. Anything above that represents boom growth, and is attractive but may be unsustainable.

Often, whole regions or groups move in cycles together. The European Union pretty much experienced a simultaneous recession in the late 1980s. Curiously, the English-speaking economies and the non-English speaking economies often move countercyclically to each other. One great advantage to exporters is that if a poor economy at home is causing sagging sales, because of the portfolio effect, the economic cycle is often better in some foreign markets.

Many organizations forecast economic growth in the various countries; among them is:

Organization for Economic Cooperation and Development (OECD)
2, rue André-Pascal
75775 Paris CEDEX 16
FRANCE
telephone: +33-1-45-24-82-00
fax: +33-1-45-24-85-00
http://www.oecd.org

Economic trends should be studied at least quarterly to help you to shape the planning and execution of your export program.

Once you are in a country, do not pull out at the first recession. International trade requires patience. Take advantage of reduced competition. Be aggressive. Acquire weaker players. Wait it out. One of the key advantages of the export strategy is the portfolio effect. Seldom is the whole world in recession at the same time. Focus resources on the growing markets while keeping your operations viable in the weak ones.

Customs Duties

All goods shipped between countries are potentially subject to customs duties. These are taxes based on the value of the articles and are collected from the recipient of the goods. The tax rates vary from zero to exorbitant depending on the category of article and the countries involved. All duties, or tariffs, are subject to the World Trade Organization's (WTO's) international multilateral tariff convention, which superseded the General Agreement on Tariffs and Trade (GATT) in 1995.

The customs officer normally uses the *commercial invoice* which must accompany each shipment to value the items. The commercial invoice is not necessarily an invoice for billing and collection purposes, but is included to make the customs job more precise. Speeding shipments through customs is the job of your shipper or customs broker. Without these expert services, shipments can tend to languish in customs for days or weeks awaiting the arrival, in person, of the intended recipient to negotiate and pay the duty, in cash. Companies such as DHL, Airborne, and Federal Express are well versed in international shipments and can help you navigate the hurdles of customs. In a few countries, mainly Italy and in South America, it may be necessary to ship via a non-U.S.-based carrier to avoid customs hassles.

The most significant and favorable factor involving software export is that, for most countries, most of the time, software is valued at the cost of the media, not the content. Thus a $10,000 software product shipped on a $5 tape is valued at $5 for the purposes of calculating the duty.

Some countries make a distinction between single master copies of software for end-user reproduction for use within the country, and multiple, shrink-wrapped, ready-for-market products. Only the latter would attract the higher, content-based resale price. This factor alone may determine whether you duplicate and ship, or ship and duplicate.

The country of origin, as well as the destination, determines the duty rate. Within the European Union (EU), for instance, all shipments are theoretically duty-free. Some European countries, notably Italy, are less predictable about how they will value software for customs, and are, as of this writing, attempting to codify which software products fall into which categories. A possible solution for this problem is to ship masters to another, more predictable EU jurisdiction, such as the Netherlands or the United Kingdom, duplicate there and ship on to their ultimate EU destination duty-free. Another approach would be to use electronic distribution.

It is usual to require the importer to pay the customs duty, and your distribution contracts should reflect this.

Withholding Tax

Many foreign governments collect a withholding tax on royalties sent out of the country. This tax is a percentage of the sale price, and will be paid directly to the government by your distributor or subsidiary. The foreign government will document receipt of this tax. If there is a tax treaty in place between the exporting country and the withholding country, the exporting country government will usually give full credit for the foreign withholdings against your domestic income tax. These withholding taxes are generally creditable against U.S. income taxes, and can be carried forward five years.

Of course you would rather have use of the money, and you may not be paying sufficient tax to use up the foreign tax credits. Withholding tax is not a good thing for export trade, but is a fact of life. For software products, as of this writing, the following withholding rates are in effect for payments to the United States. *These are examples only, not a complete list, and are subject to change:*

Representative Software Royalty
Withholding Tax Rates

JURISDICTION	TAX RATE
Australia	10%
Brazil	25%
Chile	35%
Israel	15%
Italy	10%
Japan	10%
Mexico	15%
Peru	10%
South Africa	12%
South Korea	16.125%
Taiwan	20%
Spain	10%

It is possible to reduce effective rates by exporting from your foreign subsidiary rather than your home country headquarters in some cases. Consult your accountants or lawyers for detailed advice on these subjects.

FSCs

The Taxpayer Relief Act and the Balanced Budget Act of 1997 for the first time extended the benefits of the Foreign Sales Corporation (FSC) to software companies. FSC rules are intended through tax incentives to assist U.S. companies to compete abroad with firms that may enjoy more favorable tax treatment. The tax benefit amounts to approximately 15 percent on income attributable to export sales. Consult your attorney for details.

Availability of Infrastructure

National infrastructure availability will influence the decision on when to enter a market, and will affect the cost of doing business there. Many lesser-developed countries have outmoded and expensive telephone systems, where the wait for a new connection might be months or even years. The Internet may not be freely available. The postal system may be unreliable. Transportation might be a problem, with poor roads, frequent traffic jams, and lack of public alternatives. Lagos, Nigeria, for instance, has an almost perpetual citywide traffic jam.

Europe's air transportation is notoriously expensive, despite EU deregulation. A typical intra-European flight often costs more than a trans-Atlantic one, courtesy of the international price-fixing cartel IATA (International Air Travel Association), and government jealousy in protecting flag carriers. Usually, only the national airlines of the origin and destination serve any given international route. Domestic travel in Europe can also be very dear. Flights between England and Scotland, for instance, can cost more than those between Los Angeles and New York.

In mid-1996, Germany "opened its skies" to foreign competition. It is not yet clear how much effect this has had on prices.

Productivity versus Automation

If your products are bought primarily because of the labor they save, then countries with very low labor costs, especially if skilled and highly trained people are readily available there, will probably not make good markets. India, China, and to a certain extent, Ireland, are good examples of such markets. If your products accomplish tasks which people cannot readily do, then your products should be salable there. These same markets can incidentally be good places in which to develop software.

POLITICAL FACTORS

Political stability obviously affects doing business in a country. Sudden changes in government or government policy may reduce or even completely destroy your market. A coup by an anticapitalistic faction may cost you, at least temporarily, your investment in the channel and perhaps also any ongoing maintenance stream. A revolution may close a country to business. When the Shah of Iran was deposed by Islamic forces in 1979, most commerce with the West was abruptly shut off. What had been a thriving, oil-fueled market pretty much stopped. Some companies later figured out how to do some business there, but on a much reduced scale. Today, U.S. companies are essentially banned by law from trading with Iran.

Legal Considerations

Many laws and regulations can affect U.S. business trading abroad. The following are those most likely to be encountered in software export:

Export Administration Regulations

The U.S. Department of Commerce, through the Export Administration Regulations, restricts the export of U.S. software to certain countries, imposing both civil and criminal penalties for violation. Many software products may be exported to friendly countries under export license exceptions set forth at 15 CFR Section 740.8 (Technology and Software Unrestricted), 15 CFR Section 740.3(c) (Civil End-Users), and 15 CFR Section 740.3(d) (Technology and Software Under Restriction). In certain cases, exporters may be required to obtain End-User Certificates that the foreign buyer will not re-export the software without proper authorization. Distribution contracts and end-user licenses should reflect acknowledgment of such prohibition.

Some software is restricted from export. For example, certain types of encryption software have in the past been virtually unexportable. (At the time of this writing, however, the Department of Commerce is in the process of implementing regulations to license the export of nonmilitary software with encryption capabilities incorporating the fifty-six-bit Data Encryption Standard [DES] algorithm.) Numerically controlled machine programming is also sensitive.

Export regulations apply not only to exports to end users or channel partners, but to foreign affiliates of U.S. companies, sales by your foreign affiliate within that country, and sales by your foreign affiliate to third countries. Software may be deemed exported if it is disclosed to foreign nationals in the United States, whether or not they are domestic or foreign employees of your company. Posting information on a public computer network may be deemed exporting.

The restrictions may be applicable to certain countries or to all countries. There is a complex set of criteria that determine the classification of software into these categories. These rules are available from the U.S. Department of Commerce (see Table 3.1). You may apply these rules yourself or ask the Department of Commerce to give a ruling. There is a nominal charge for each ruling, which requires a number of weeks for issuance.

Even if you do not need an export license, U.S. exporters are often required under the Export Administration Regulations to, among other duties, comply with record-keeping requirements and file Shipper's Export Declarations.

Unfortunately, the Department of Commerce has been a little slow (by its own admission) in reflecting the end of the Cold War in these rules. Most annoying to foreign customers is the necessity of the non-re-export undertaking (though this may be part of a shrink-wrap license).

You must pay strict attention in complying with export controls. The penalties for violation include prison terms of up to ten years. But despite their potentially daunting nature, once the procedure is established for compliance, the process can be completely routine. For a more in-depth discussion of export licensing, see Maggiori's *How to Make the World Your Market.*

Table 3.1. Regulations Changes

For the first time in more than forty years, the U.S. government in 1996 completed a major revision in export regulations. The 1996 edition of *Export Administration Regulations* is available from the Superintendent of Documents.

This publication contains the most current rules which control the export of dual-use commodities, technology, and software, and includes features that make the regulations easier to understand. Subscribers receive up-to-date, authoritative information on current export licensing requirements, including: how to obtain an export license; when an export license is required; how license applications are reviewed; current policy changes; new restrictions on selected commodities and on exports to certain countries; and where to get assistance.

Subscriptions are $88 and can be obtained by calling +1-202-512-1800, fax +1-202-512-2250. Orders must reference publication code EAR96. Mastercard and Visa orders are accepted by phone and fax. Mail orders must include credit card information or a check payable to Superintendent of Documents. Send order to:

Superintendent of Documents
P.O. Box 371954
Pittsburgh, PA 15250-7954

These regulations may also be viewed on-line at: *http://www.access/gpo.gov/doc/index.html*

The U.S. Department of Commerce also operates an automated phone service at the Bureau of Export Administration (BXA). The Export Licensing Voice Information System (ELVIS) offers a wide range of licensing information and emergency procedures. Through ELVIS, callers may order forms and publications or subscribe to the Office of Export Licensing (OEL) *Insider Newsletter Bulletin,* which provides regulatory updates. While using ELVIS, a caller has the option to speak to a BXA consultant. You may reach ELVIS by calling +1-202-482-4811.

Trading with the Enemy and International Emergency Economic Powers Acts

Embargoes enforced by the Treasury Department under these Acts as of mid-1996 exclude trading with or establishing business operations in Libya, North Korea, Cuba, Iraq, and under certain circumstances, Iran. This list changes. There are both civil and criminal penalties.

Foreign Corrupt Practices Act

This law essentially prohibits U.S. companies, their employees, agents, distributors, and sales representatives from offering bribes to foreign government officials. A bribe is a payment of anything of value to obtain business. The law also mandates for public companies certain accounting standards related to foreign payments. There are both civil and criminal penalties.

Since bribery to obtain business is commonplace in many countries around the world, this law is probably the most likely to come into play for the U.S. exporter, especially outside Western Europe, Canada, Japan, Australia, and New Zealand. Many such second- and third-world bureaucrats depend on routine bribes to supplement their very meager salaries. On the other hand, most successful U.S. software companies happily do legal business nearly everywhere.

If you are a U.S. resident, you simply cannot get involved in bribing officials, or you could personally go to jail. Well-known companies such as IBM and Raytheon have been involved in well-publicized accusations regarding corruption in South America in recent years.

It is best to have clear, unambiguous corporate standards prohibiting bribery. These standards should be disseminated and understood throughout the distribution channel. Your attorney should be able to help you set up a set of procedures to investigate and then obligate all your foreign agents to comply with U.S. laws. In the event one of them fails to do so, you will have the defense that you have taken all reasonable steps to comply.

Incidentally, the United States is the only country to have a law of this nature. Your foreign competitors have only their consciences to keep them honest. In fact, many countries permit the cost of foreign bribes to be deducted as a business expense from income taxes.

In February 1996, *Entrepreneur* magazine reported the 1995 Corruption Index, resulting from a survey of international business executives around the globe. The Index showed Pakistan, China, and Indonesia to be the most corrupt countries in the world. New Zealand, Denmark, and Singapore were considered least corrupt.

Arms Export Control Act

Administered by the State Department, the International Traffic in Arms Regulations (ITARs) under this act prohibit exports of products on the U.S. Munitions List without a license. Encryption software is on this list. Civil and criminal penalties exist.

Until August, 1995, merely traveling abroad with a notebook computer on which a covered encryption routine resided was a violation of this act. Now, if purely for personal use, such an action is usually permissible. No foreign national may have access to the computer, and it must be under your control at all times. No copies may be made.

Antiboycott Laws

Now that there is movement in an Arab-Israeli peace process, and Palestinians within Israel have a degree of self-governance, the anti-Israel boycott is no longer the problem it once was for U.S. businesses. Under U.S. law, if a U.S. company is asked by a foreign customer or prospect to boycott Israel or to show that it does not do business with Israel, such a request may not legally be complied with, and the request itself must be reported to both the Commerce and Treasury Departments. This situation now arises rarely, but is not unknown.

Note that the above section on Legal Considerations is far from a complete description of the relevant laws. Consulting a knowledgeable U.S. export attorney is highly advisable.

Foreign Law

The preceding Legal Considerations concerned U.S. laws. If you establish a trading entity abroad, that entity and its employees are subject to the laws of the jurisdiction in which they trade. You must know and operate within these laws. Advice from local counsel is essential.

Advertising

Advertising comparing your product favorably to a competitor's is illegal in most of Europe unless accompanied by documented proof. Fath points out in *How to Develop and Manage Successful Distributor Channels in World Markets* some other advertising traps abroad:

> In Saudi Arabia, women may be shown only in ads for female products. In some countries you may not advertise a selling price; in others you *must* advertise a selling price. In many Asian markets you cannot advertise unless your product is available in the market and your ad informs your consumers where they can purchase the product. (pp. 28-29)

Intellectual Property Protection

Your software products are very likely your company's primary assets. These must be protected with great diligence throughout the world. Both channel and end user contract provisions in each territory should attempt to provide protection comparable to what the company enjoys domestically.

There are four categories of concern for intellectual property: copyrights, trade secrets, patents, and trademarks.

Copyrights

International protection is available for copyrights in many foreign countries under the Bern Convention. In many countries registration is not required to obtain a copyright. It is sufficient to place the notice, *"Copyright © 1998 Vendor Inc.,"* conspicuously on the work. This includes manuals, screen displays, tape and disk labels, and other media to be protected.

Certain countries, although Bern signatories, have notably weak enforcement and a resulting proliferation of piracy, which will be discussed later in this chapter.

Trade Secrets

Trade secrets are a concept of U.S. state law, and may not be enforceable in certain foreign countries. It is possible to obtain trade secret protection with foreign parties in certain jurisdictions through contractual means. It may be your policy to license and export only object code so as to protect the trade secret source code. This policy can be maintained even when a distributor is performing language translation, as the translations are of screens and messages only, which can be made available separately from the program logic, if properly designed.

Patents

U.S. patents are likewise not valid outside the United States, and must be applied for and obtained in each foreign jurisdiction. In the European Union, however, a single patent application may be made for the entire Union, although fees must be paid for each country registered.

Trademarks

Trademark registration must also be pursued in each country of interest. Note that unlike the United States, most countries follow a "first registration" rather than a "first use" rule. Thus, if you do not register your trademarks you may fall prey to "trademark pirates" who register many marks and then attempt to sell them to their actual users. (In more than one case, a software company discovered, upon attempting to terminate a distribution agreement, that their distributor, not they, owned the trademarks in the territory.) Registration of multiple marks in multiple countries is expensive (roughly U.S. $250 to $1,000 each). If your product is hot, or well-known, you would be well-advised to register early. If it is not, you may not have a problem.

A single registration will also suffice in the EU, though a trademark search in each country of desired protection must be made. Your attorney will apply to the EU Trademark Office in Allicante, Spain.

Channel partners are usually granted limited rights to use the owner's trademarks, subject to approval, always identifying them as belonging to the company. You must assure yourself that the marks are being properly used: correct fonts, styles, and so forth. If not, the marks can be blurred and eventually lost. Each first use of a registered trademark on a piece must be designated with the ® symbol. If the mark is unregistered, use the ™ symbol. Using ® for an unregistered mark may be considered fraud by the patent and trademark office.

Strong and Weak Protection Territories

As of this writing, the following markets generally offer relatively strong intellectual property protection environments for software:

- Australia
- Austria
- The Benelux countries
- Canada
- Germany
- Ireland
- New Zealand
- The Nordic countries
- Switzerland
- The United Kingdom
- The United States

whereas the following are currently problematical:

- China
- Italy
- Hong Kong
- Korea

To obtain a current list of such problem countries, contact:

Office of the U.S. Trade Representative
Winder Bldg.
600 17th St. NW
Washington, DC 20508

telephone: +1-202-395-3000

Despite the protections afforded by registration, full contractual protection for all intellectual property should be obtained in each country, both from the channel partners and through approved sub-license agreements, from the end users.

Some relevant case studies (and some quite entertaining recent history) of software intellectual property disputation may be found in Anthony Lawrence Clapes' *Softwars: The Legal Battles for Control of the Global Software Industry.*

Piracy

Software piracy worldwide is a big problem for all software companies. But just because a country is known to be lax in enforcing its intellectual property laws, do not automatically consider this a reason not to export to that country. Here's why:

Your product can be pirated in a country whether or not you choose to legally distribute there. All the pirate has to do is to legally obtain a copy of your product in a country you do distribute in, take it to the lax jurisdiction, and begin selling illegal copies. Your being present in such lax jurisdictions with legitimate distribution can actually *reduce* such piracy, considering the following:

- Some local users will wish to legally purchase the rights to use your product. If you deny them that opportunity, they may feel forced to buy from pirates.
- Some users want to deal with the legitimate vendor so as to obtain the best possible service. Pirates probably will not be able to supply this.
- If you have a distribution channel in the country, that channel itself will act to try to enforce any intellectual property rights (though admittedly weak) that may exist locally.
- You can compete with the pirates. You cannot compete on price, but you can eliminate any natural monopoly you may have granted by staying out of the market and thus cut their market share to less than 100 percent.

Personal Safety and Insurance

It is not physically safe to visit certain places. If you stand out visibly from the local populace, you may also be at risk in some countries. These places are few, and hardly ever in first-world countries. The U.S. government also bans most travel by its citizens to places like North Korea and Cuba.

The U.S. Department of State maintains a travel advisory hot line: +1-202-647-5225. Considerable information including travel safety assessments are available from this twenty-four-hour service. It is also possible to download this information in digital form. Refer to this and other available information to determine whether travel should be planned to doubtful destinations.

Apart from the obvious concern for one's physical welfare, there may be other reasons to avoid traveling to dangerous destinations. Check with your insurance carrier to see what countries may be on its list of prohibited destinations.

It is safer in general not to advertise that one is a U.S. citizen when traveling abroad. Luggage tags should not be readable by a casual observer. The cut and color of one's clothing, hair style, and other factors are also telltale to the experienced observer. This is merely background information. It is neither necessary nor desirable to become a spy to travel and work safely abroad. Perhaps the most useful advice is to be constantly aware of your surroundings when in public. Notice who and what are around you, and do not be lulled into a false sense of security just because you are in an exotic city. All common crimes can occur anywhere in the world.

On the other hand, some places are quite a bit safer than others. Japan, Australia, New Zealand, and Singapore are noted as particularly safe destinations for the law-abiding visitor.

See Herman J. Maggiori's *How to Make the World Your Market* on traveling safely and protecting yourself against terrorism abroad.

Other Personal Considerations

In some cases, you may choose not to do business in a country, even though it can be done legally. Many U.S. firms chose not to do any business in South Africa in the days of apartheid, purely out of personal, ethical considerations, even though U.S. federal law made illegal only investment and selling to apartheid-enforcing agencies. One might have the same feelings today about doing business with certain countries.

ISO 9000/9001

The International Standards Organization (ISO) has issued and maintains a family of quality standards referred to as ISO 9000. The subset of that family which most directly applies to the software industry is ISO 9001.

ISO has more weight in Europe than elsewhere, but a significant number of U.S. software companies have adopted the ISO 9001 standard. Adoption is time-consuming and expensive. It involves hiring ISO-certified consultants who will both work with your firm to establish the quality procedures, and then, when the procedures are implemented to their satisfaction, issue the certification. This initial process generally takes six to eighteen months. In order to maintain the certification, it must thereafter be periodically revalidated by an objective third party.

ISO 9001 certification consists basically of analyzing and documenting the exact processes your organization follows (or should follow) to correctly develop and produce its products, then putting procedures in place to assure that those documented processes are consistently followed. Implementation is a significant task for most organizations, and *will* have organizational impacts and costs in resources.

Many European Union governments have mandated that all their suppliers, and those suppliers' suppliers (and so on) be ISO certified. To date, this is not rigorously enforced in most countries. However, certification could give your company a competitive edge if you are competing for a lot of government business. In Europe, the certification also has some cachet among customers in certain industries, and does definitely indicate that you value quality highly enough to go through the pain and expense of certification.

Even putting the time and expense of certification aside, there are mixed feelings among U.S. software vendors regarding ISO 9000. The standard was initially designed for manufacturing processes, which we know clearly that software development is not. But perhaps its biggest weakness is that this standard has to do only with process repeatability, and does not itself actually mandate the measurement and tracking to quality. So if your current procedures followed precisely yield a poor quality product now, they will be certain to do so after ISO 9001 is in place.

In late 1995, the Japanese government proposed that all software imported into Japan be ISO 9001 certified. This policy was viewed by the U.S. government as overtly protectionist, and was quickly dropped by Japan. If you should decide not to proceed with ISO standards now, it will pay to keep an eye on developments in this arena in the future.

THE EUROPEAN UNION

The European Union is the world's largest trading bloc, with an affluent population of 370 million. In 1957, the Treaty of Rome created an economic bloc of six Western European nations. Over the subsequent forty years, this group has grown both more comprehensive in scope and to cover almost all of Western Europe in geography. Now known as the European Union (EU), the bloc was first known as the European Economic Community (EEC) and later as the European Community (EC). Since Western Europe is likely to comprise a major market for most software companies, some knowledge of the EU will be helpful.

Today, fifteen nations make up the European Union: Austria, Belgium, Denmark, Finland, France, Germany, Greece, Ireland, Italy, Luxembourg, the Netherlands, Portugal, Spain, Sweden, and the United Kingdom. Notably absent are Switzerland and Norway, which have their own reasons for wishing to remain economically independent.

The EU's administrative headquarters are in Brussels, its legislative bodies meet in Strasbourg, France, and the Court of Justice of the European Communities in Luxembourg serves as its judicial arm.

The principal goal of the EU is implementation of the "four freedoms": enabling people, goods, services, and money to move freely within the Union. This goal has resulted in the elimination of trade barriers including customs duties, nonuniform standards for goods and services, border formalities, and the like. The motive is to create a strong economic trading bloc to compete with the United States and Japan. The formation of the North American Free Trade Agreement (NAFTA) has added impetus to complete the union, which is still incomplete in many respects.

The EU comprises a market with an aggregate gross national product (GNP) comparable to that of the United States. Forty percent of all the world's merchandise trade, and 55 percent of its trade in services, is between the United States and Europe. A goal of the

EU is a single currency by the end of the millennium. This difficult and elusive goal will be met only if member states can adhere to strict economic formulas designed to prevent their individual currencies from inflating too fast. It now appears unlikely that more than a few members will be able to participate in a single currency by the target date. Another goal is a common defense, which, as events in Bosnia proved, is sorely lacking. (Further information on the EU's structure and principles can be found in publications from the Office of Official Publications of the European Communities, particularly: *The Single Market;* and *Serving the European Union: A Citizen's Guide to the Institutions of the European Union.*)

The 1995 European market for information technology infrastructure was U.S. $169 billion, the largest regional market outside the United States according to U.S. Department of Commerce publication, *The European Information Marketplace: Technology, Infrastructure and Services.*

Be cautioned that the EU is emphatically *not* a country. The differences in language, culture, and currency among the member states far exceed the similarities of legal superstructure of the Union. A marketing approach that works well in Spain, for instance, may fail completely in Germany. A French salesman will have a difficult time selling in the United Kingdom, and vice-versa.

There are actually few direct implications for companies exporting software into the EU. Undue competition from local firms is not to be expected, except in a few cases of favoritism toward national companies when awarding government contracts for custom software services. "Quality rules in Europe," said Charles Ludolph, Director of European Union and Regional Affairs, U.S. Department of Commerce, at the 1996 Virginia Conference on World Trade. According to Ludolph, of the three principal product differentiators, quality, price, and availability, quality is in Europe the "top competitive factor, availability next and price last." This may be different than in North American markets.

A few member states, such as Italy and Portugal, are stricter in interpreting customs regulations and have higher tariffs for external goods than others. This can sometimes result in long delays in customs and seemingly punitive duties being levied, especially if apparently immaterial import and shipping procedures are not carried out exactly in the prescribed manner. One way of avoiding these problems is to establish a distribution center in a more trade-friendly member state. EU countries which actively encourage the formation of such centers include the Netherlands, Denmark, and the United Kingdom. Representatives of these governments will work with you to avoid most customs hassles. Once your products are in the EU, they can then be transshipped to any other EU destination without the further involvement of customs.

Legal and Financial

Each country has its own unique laws, customs, and business practices. These must be understood and incorporated into any successful business venture there. Sources of information include consultants, international lawyers, and accountants.

Civil Law versus Common Law Practices

Common law is the unwritten law of legal precedents which forms the basis of the legal system in the United Kingdom, where it originated, and in many of its former colonies. Not satisfied with the vague, uncodified nature of common law, Napoleon introduced a system of published statues known as the Napoleonic Code. Later known as Civil Law, this approach is taken in jurisdictions formerly dominated by Napoleon, including France, Spain, Italy, and curiously, what is now the state of Louisiana.

Standard Contract Considerations

In consultation with your counsel, develop a standard set of distribution contracts for use in your business. This initial effort will repay you many times. Perhaps your set of agreements will include a distribution agreement for EU countries (whose laws are particular and restrictive), one for non-EU countries, a master VAR agreement, a preliminary nondisclosure agreement, and an end user license agreement for direct foreign license sales. See Appendix 3 for an example of a distribution agreement. Also see Fath's compilation of EU laws governing distributor relations in *How to Develop and Manage Successful Distributor Channels in World Markets.*

Unless your products require extensive, in-the-field customization, license and export only object code so as to protect the trade secret source code.

Be conscious of the constraints of local law. France requires contracts between local parties (such as a sublicense agreement of a local distributor) to be in French. German law requires a minimum six-month warranty. Prudence dictates that foreign contracts not be entered into without reviews by both domestic and local foreign legal counsel.

When modifications to your standard agreement are called for—either for reasons of compliance to local law, during initial negotiations, or subsequently during the course of business—use consecutively-numbered amendments, rather than directly modifying the body of the text itself. This will save you countless hours and many mistakes in later interpretation of the agreements.

Antitrust

The EU enforces laws against the restraint of trade. As they affect software distribution, these laws prohibit parties from entering into exclusive distribution agreements within the Union. Permissible is the restriction against marketing or soliciting orders outside an agreed territory, but a distributor may not be contractually prevented from accepting a bona fide order from any potential customer in the EU. In practice, this legal structure is not too troublesome. By restricting solicitation, the semblance of exclusivity can be maintained quite successfully, if exclusivity is desired.

There are also laws against price fixing. You may not dictate the prices at which your distributor or VAR resells sublicenses for your products to end-users within the EU. This should not be a major problem either, as you *are* permitted to set a minimum royalty or license fee which the channel partner must pay you for the products. This will in effect limit discounting if that is your intent.

Territories

The big four European markets are Germany, France, the United Kingdom, and Italy. In 1995, the European information technology market was 28 percent in Germany, 17 percent in France, 16 percent in the United Kingdom, and 8 percent in Italy, according to *Euro-*

pean Information Technology Observatory 96. Go after them first. Then add the Benelux (Belgium, Netherlands, and Luxembourg), Iberia (Spain and Portugal), and the Nordic countries (Nordic denotes Denmark, Norway, Sweden, and Finland, whereas Scandinavia does not include Finland). If you divide Switzerland by language groups and associate them appropriately with Germany, France, and Italy, and add Austria to the German-speaking territory, you will have seven territories covering most of Western Europe. (Add Japan, Brazil, and Australia/New Zealand, and you will have ten manageable territories covering over 80 percent of the computer market outside North America, according to *Worldwide Information Technology Market* 1995 market data.) (See Table 3.2 for information on the European information technology markets.)

JAPAN AS A SPECIAL CASE

Although each country and culture is unique, Japan seems, to the Westerner, more different than most. It is here, where exists nearly 20 percent of the world's computer market, that Western firms attempting to export often stumble and fail without quite knowing why. There are many good books about doing business in Japan. Read one or two before you visit.

Theory Z by William G. Ouchi is excellent not only in understanding the Japanese, but in learning how to apply some of their most powerful principles to your own organization. Hiroki and Joan Kato have nicely catalogued the key characteristics of business culture in Japan in their very readable *Understanding and Working with the Japanese Business World.*

But reading books will not fully prepare you for the important nuances. These are learned only "on the ground." It really pays to have an ally (preferably an employee) who speaks the language fluently, and knows the customs.

Japanese Business Culture

The Japanese company is a more significant institution in the life of its typical employee than is the Western one. Typically all hiring is done of new graduates, once a year. They all join in an impressive

Table 3.2. European Information Technology and Information Services Market

Territory	1995 IT Market $U.S. billions	1994-1995 Market Growth %
Austria	3.8	7.5
Belgium/Luxembourg	5.3	3.8
Denmark	4.2	9.2
Finland	2.4	11.8
France	28.2	5.4
Germany	47.7	7.4
Greece	0.7	11.7
Ireland	0.9	6.5
Italy	14.5	5.3
Netherlands	9.6	8.5
Norway	3.3	9.4
Portugal	1.0	6.3
Spain	6.1	7.4
Sweden	6.1	12.6
Switzerland	7.6	8.4
United Kingdom	27.4	8.9
Europe	168.9	7.5

Source: European Information Technology Observatory, *EITO 96,* Frankfurt-Main, Germany, 1996.

formal ceremony. Thereafter, they may spend twelve hours a day there, five or six days a week, for many years.

Management titles such as *hacho* and *bucho* are military ranks, too: hierarchy and seniority are much more important than brilliance and creativity.

Japanese are good businessmen. (Almost all businesspeople are men. The system in nearly every company prevents women from rising to positions of responsibility.) They have built one of the world's foremost export economies by selling their goods and services all over the world, even in countries where, for historical reasons, the citizens may dislike them.

Japanese business has succeeded largely because of two things: quality and service. These might sound like clichés to the American ear, but they mean something very specific to the Japanese. Not only does Japan sell quality and service, but it fully expects to *buy* quality and service. And is willing to pay for them. But provide poor quality and limited service, and the market will close to you for a long time. The saying goes, "Americans send faxes—Japanese send engineers." And that is the heart of it.

Three keys to success in Japan are reputation, introduction, and relationship. Your reputation is very important in Japan. If your company is already known there, great. If not, be prepared to show that you have established a reputation elsewhere.

You will not get to see the people you need to see without the proper introduction from someone who does have a good reputation with those people. The U.S. Embassy may be able to help here, or a supplier, hardware manufacturer, or other business partner.

Then you must build the relationship. That may mean not talking much business in the first meeting. More important are going out to dinner, sharing traditional foods, drinking a lot of sake with the traditional Japanese toast, *"kampai,"* loudly given, and making fools of yourselves singing *karaoke*. The restraints of Japanese business fall away with alcohol, people are more honest, and this is when bonding can be done.

When your Japanese counterparts visit you, show them a good time. Take them somewhere photogenic, because they will likely have their cameras. Many Japanese businessmen would enjoy going to a shooting range and firing rifles or pistols. This experience is not available in Japan. Golf is also very popular among Japanese, and very expensive at home.

Several visits, back and forth, would typically be required, over a period of months or even years for enough trust to be established to begin a significant business relationship. This is not typically the Western way, but maybe it should be!

Japan is a crowded island. In learning to live together in very close quarters, often with only rice-paper walls separating families, ritual politeness became an important virtue early in the nation's history. Open disagreement is not part of Japanese culture. A Japanese person simply will not say "no" to your proposal. If you get a "maybe not" that definitely means "no way."

Please do not conclude from this discussion that Japanese people are tricky, deceptive, or unkind. They are a fine people with a proud heritage, a thousand-year-old culture, and world-class accomplishments. You can make close Japanese friends in time who will treat you with kindness and generosity you have never experienced elsewhere. They behave according to their culture, just as we all do. It is the Western visitor who may be confused or may misinterpret. But that is the visitor's responsibility.

The Software Business

Customers in Japan, other than consumers, do not expect to install software themselves. The seller must do that, both the original release, and all upgrades. If the product is complex, critical, or less than stable, the seller will be expected to be on site *every day* until the customer is comfortable.

Japan is the least tolerant market to non-nationalized software (excepting of course the United States and all other English-speaking countries). Translating the manuals is considered a minimum for industrial products. Full "Japanization" is required for all consumer products and many others as well. It is, however, possible to get started in Japan without a localized version, selling at first to only foreign multinationals. This will give you some time to Japanize the product, while still getting some revenue from the territory.

The cost of this approach is borne at least partially, and often fully, by your distribution partner in the country, who will probably insist on a lower royalty or higher discount than normal to compensate, as well as exclusivity to protect his investment. Be prepared to negotiate, but be realistic. The cost of doing business here is higher. The margin will have to come from some combination of higher prices and lower cost of goods. Discounts of up to 25 percent higher than elsewhere are routinely given to Japanese distribution partners.

The Japanese prospect, even more than the European one, and much more than the American, is interested in quantifiable benefits from software. They will seldom buy on "sizzle," marketing hype, current buzzwords, brilliant architecture, or distant futures. The way to sell commercial software in Japan is to come prepared with verifiable stories of five to ten internationally-known companies who have used your product and have concrete, quantified savings, or productivity increases to show for it. Selling consumer software in Japan is tougher. Home computers are much less widespread, and they are less common in businesses than elsewhere.

To type in *kanji*, or Japanese characters, you first have to press the key for the character that sounds like the one you want. The screen then displays a menu of many possible homonymous characters, from which you then must choose the right one. If this seems tedious, it is. The demographics reflect this. According to 1995 figures from International Data Corporation, *Worldwide Information Technology Market*, the market value ratio in Japan for single-user systems versus multiuser computers is 1:1. In the rest of the world, it is about 2:1. In the United States it is nearly 3:1.

Protocol

Address Japanese by their family names with *"san"* added at the end, meaning roughly "Mr." or "Ms." This is the way they address each other in business. Like the Germans and the French, they probably cannot even recall the given names of their business colleagues, because given names are never used in business.

Meishi

When you visit Japan, have some two-sided, bilingual business cards made up. A good Japanese hotel can do this for you from your English card in twenty-four hours. Present your card *(meishi)* with both hands, Japanese side up, readable to the person you are meeting. Receive his card with both hands, too. Then study the card. To immediately put his card in your pocket is an insult. Besides, you might learn something valuable from the card. (Note: Do not ever give your Japanese *meishi* to other than a Japanese. To give one to a Korean or Chinese would be an insult.)

Omiagi

Be prepared to present a small gift when meeting a Japanese in Japan. The visitor is always expected to bring *omiagi* and present it upon arrival. You should have something for each person, with the best gift for the boss. Do not spend too much shopping here—it is the thought that counts. Something with your company logo, or from your home region is best. Golf shirts and liquor, especially scotch and whiskey, are also appreciated.

Tables versus Text

Japanese businesspeople tend to communicate by writing in tabular or matrix form. They are accustomed to seeing a business case or proposal laid out in rows and columns, even in situations where a Westerner would use text. Conform to that style and communicate more effectively.

Laughter

Laughter in a business setting often indicates nervousness or anxiety. If you inspire laughs during a meeting, it is not because you are amusing, but because you have embarrassed someone (probably yourself, though you have not realized it yet).

Consensus

Japanese tend to decide by consensus. This means decisions may take longer, but once made, will have the full weight of the organization behind them. Patience counts.

JETRO

You can get free office space in Japan to help you in getting your export program started there. The Japan External Trade Organization (JETRO) maintains a number of Business Support Centers (BSCs) in Japan. These centers function as temporary strategic bases for private companies making an initial market approach.

Each facility provides everything needed to carry out initial market development in Japan. The BSCs incorporate a number of private offices, each containing a desk, chairs, cabinet space, a phone, a facsimile machine and a word processor. Additionally, computer stations, libraries, help desks, advisors, and meeting halls are available. JETRO maintains a database which contains extensive data about potential importers, best-selling products, trade fairs, and other market-related information.

There are five regional JETRO centers in the United States: New York City, Chicago, Atlanta, Los Angeles, and San Francisco, and seventy-nine in other countries. In addition, there are JETRO Senior Trade Advisors in the following U.S. states: MI, IN, OH, MN, MO, WI, MA, NY, NC, TN, OR, WA, AZ, CA, SC, FL, TX, LA, OK, and NB. You can find their coordinates on the web at *http://www.jetro.org* or by calling +1-212-764-4200. Contact headquarters directly at:

JETRO Head Office
Import Promotion Department
2-5, 2 Chome
Toranomon
Minato-ku
Tokyo 105
Japan

telephone: +81-3-3582-5173
fax: +81-3-5572-7044

Ashisuto

K.K. Ashisuto (the "K.K." is the rough Japanese equivalent to "Inc.," and Ashisuto is pronounced as if the "u" was not present) is Japan's largest reseller of foreign software. They have major relationships with Computer Associates and Oracle, and dozens of smaller firms. KKA was founded by Dr. Bill Totten, an American economist, but is otherwise staffed by Japanese. Contact their Tokyo headquarters as follows:

K.K. Ashisuto
3-1-1 Toranomon
Minato-ku
Tokyo 105
JAPAN

telephone: +81-3-3437-0651
fax: +81-3-3437-0758
http://www.ashisuto.co.jp

Computing Japan

Computing Japan is a monthly publication devoted to the Japanese computer market. It features mostly PC and Internet editorial content, but helps spell out the entire software market milieu in Japan. For subscription information, contact *Computing Japan* at the following:

in the United States:

P.O. Box 547
Midpines, CA 95347

telephone: +1-209-742-4252
telephone U.S. only: 1-800-330-5822
fax: +1-209-966-8406
http://www.cjmag.co.jp

in Japan:

5 Wako Bldg.
19-8 Kakigara-cho
1 Chome
Nihonbashi
Chuoku
Tokyo 103
JAPAN

telephone: +81-3-3661-8373
fax: +81-3-3667-9646
e-mail: subs@cjmag.co.jp

HOMEWORK—SOURCES

Information about the foreign software markets and their in-place distribution channels may be found at home and abroad. Doing research at home is obviously cheaper in terms of time and travel costs, and is good preparation for the in-country field work that follows.

Other Software Companies

Many software companies, including your competitors and other players in your application space, will disclose through their World Wide Web (www) sites their foreign channel partners. Often there are links to channel partner sites, making preliminary research through the Internet very productive. Other sources include software company brochures, ads, information from reader response cards, annual reports, and 10Ks.

If a competitor is weak, you may wish to recruit away portions of his distribution channel. (Though if successful you may question the long-term loyalty of your new partner.) It is better to discover how products which are complementary to yours are distributed. If a channel is reaching the same buyers, you may have a natural match in a channel partner.

Hardware Vendors

Most hardware vendors are happy to help suppliers of software that runs on their machines. Software sells hardware, and hardware vendors try hard to have an extensive library of software offerings available to their customers worldwide. They therefore will often make available market numbers and might make introductions to possible channel partners. Though installed base numbers may be available from hardware or software vendors, do not be surprised if this information is considered proprietary.

Alliances

Many major hardware and software firms offer alliances and partnerships to providers of compatible software products. Sun Microsystems, Hewlett Packard, IBM, Digital Equipment, NCR,

Computer Associates, Microsoft, Oracle, Sybase, and Informix all support one or more such organizations. It may be possible through these programs to obtain local introductions, customer lists, mailing and seminar participation, invitations to attend or exhibit worldwide at user conferences, and derivative memberships in local chapters in foreign countries.

Microsoft InfoSource is a worldwide CD-ROM directory of solution providers and resellers, searchable by country, product, and platform. Its catalog number is: 1295-098-6285 CD WIN InfoSource. Though normally available only to Microsoft Solution Providers, if your product is Microsoft-compatible, you can easily become one.

Market Research Companies

Well-known firms such as Gartner Group, IDC, Yankee Group, Input, and Meta Group in the United States, and Xephon in the United Kingdom, offer research capabilities and publications that can help in many ways in software market selection and penetration. *Marketing News* publishes an annual *Directory of International Research Firms*. Though not specific to the computer field, the *Directory* lists several hundred firms located in over fifty countries. Contact:

Marketing News
250 S. Wacker Dr.
Chicago, IL 60606-5819

telephone: +1-312-831-2736
fax: +1-312-648-0103

Ideas + Information, Inc. maintains a worldwide database of international computer channels and market information, including nearly 10,000 distributors and VARs worldwide. Contact:

Ideas + Information, Inc.
P.O. Box H
Exeter, NH 03833

telephone: +1-603-394-7900
fax: +1-603-394-7601
e-mail: info@interinfo.com

International Data Corporation (IDC) publishes sister weeklies to *Computerworld* in many foreign markets. Contact them to obtain sample copies from the markets of interest, as follows:

International Data Corporation
5 Speen St.
Framingham, MA 01701

telephone: +1-508-872-8200
fax: +1-508-935-4015
http:// www.idcresearch.com

Spikes Cavell & Co. provides access to its database of corporate and government end-user software buyers in Europe. The information is available by country and by hardware platform. Contact:

Spikes Cavell & Co.
Benham Valence
Newbury
Berkshire RG20 8LU
ENGLAND

telephone: +44-1635-550-449
fax: +44-1635-463-69

Consultants

There are many small consulting firms and independent consultants with international software distribution expertise. Those which follow are far from a complete listing. A good consultant can research the market, internationalize your product, locate appropriate candidate distribution partners, help you select the right ones, and even help to manage them.

Not all the following firms would be right for you. Check them out carefully before engaging one:

Asia Software Management Resources Pte. Ltd.
5 Collman Street #B1-13
SINGAPORE 179805

telephone: +65-334-1936
fax: +65-339-1233
e-mail: asmrpte@singnet.com.sg

The EMS Group
111 Pine St. Suite 1620
San Francisco, CA 94111

telephone: +1-415-433-4344
fax: +1-415-433-4358
e-mail: calexander@emsgroup.com
http://www.emsgroup.com

EMS London
Aldwych House
Madiera Road
West Byfleet
KT14 6DA
ENGLAND

telephone: +44-1932-354-771
fax: +44-1932-355-292

Euramark
2, Impasse de la Gonnée
60800 Trumilly
FRANCE

telephone: +33-3-44-59-00-65
fax: +33-3-44-59-00-67
e-mail: euramark@compuserve.com

European IT Solutions Ltd.
Exchange Building
16 St. Cuthbert's Street
Bedford MK40 3JG
ENGLAND

telephone: +44-1234-345-049
fax: +44-1234-345-118
e-mail: exec@cits.co.uk
http://www.eits.co.uk

International Business Strategies
The Glassmill
1 Battersea Bridge Road
London SW11 3BG
ENGLAND

telephone: +44-71-924-2011
fax: +44-71-924-5851

International High-Technologies Consulting
P.O. Box 6194
Freehold, NJ 07728

telephone: +1-908-845-5481
fax: +1-908-845-5492

Open World Distribution
16345 Northeast Eugene Court
Portland, OR 97230

telephone: +1-503-252-3969
fax: +1-503-252-0748
http://www.thechannel.com

PDi—Profit Development International
216 21st Place
Santa Monica, CA 90402

telephone: +1-310-394-5775
fax: +1-310-394-6426
e-mail: richard.hannes@internet.mci.com

Sally Goodsell International Marketing
The Garden House
132 Alderney St.
London SW1 V4HA
ENGLAND

telephone: +44-171-834-4874
fax: +44-171-834-5955
e-mail: sg@international-marketing.co.uk
http://www.international-marketing.co.uk

Software International
378 Pond St.
Weymouth, MA 02190

telephone: +1-617-847-3879
fax: +1-617-331-7448

WestSoft Asia
391 Orchard Road
#12-01 Ngee Ann City Tower A
SINGAPORE 238873

telephone: +65-476-0415
fax: +65-476-1206
e-mail: westsoft@pacific.net.sg

The Internet

Searching the World Wide Web using Yahoo!, HotBot, or Alta Vista will yield a host of information, including the home pages with e-mail addresses of many potential channel partners. Correspond with them, asking about their possible interest in representing your product.

Consult the *Internet Resource Guide* of the U.S. Department of Commerce, Trade Information Center, Office of Export Promotion Coordination, Trade Development. It can be obtained by calling 1-800-USA-TRAD in the United States. It includes a listing of about 200 international trade web sites, and has been adapted for inclusion as Appendix 5.

www.krislyn.com/sites/internet.htm contains links to nearly fifty international business sites including EXIMBANK, the International Monetary Fund, National Trade Data Bank, NAFTA Register, World Trade Organization, and many country-specific sites.

Trade Publications

Consult both domestic and foreign trade publications, not only of the computer industry, but of the vertical industries you target. Industry periodicals occasionally contain market size estimates from various sources.

U.S. Department of Commerce

The U.S. government wants to promote export. Get their help from the following places:

- U.S. Government Export Information: +1-800-359-3997
- Export Administration Export Assistance: +1-202-482-4811
- U.S. Foreign and Commercial Service: +1-202-482-2000

The Department of Commerce has local field offices in most major U.S. cities, each of which will have a U.S. Foreign and Commercial Service officer on staff to assist you with your export needs. Consult a local telephone directory.

NTDB—the National Trade Databank—is available on CD ROM. It includes hundreds of thousands of entries from all over the world including potential distributors by industry. Order from:

U.S. & Foreign Service
National Technical Information Service
5385 Port Royal Road
Springfield, VA 22161

telephone: +1-703-487-4650

TradePort Export Assistance on the Internet

The following information on TradePort is an excerpt from "The International News Flash," June 1996:

TradePort, a comprehensive, electronic, interactive export assistance program, is available on the World Wide Web at http://tradeport.org. The goals of the TradePort are to provide trade services to businesses of all types and sizes, to increase U.S. exports, and to ultimately create jobs. TradePort is made possible through a partnership between various public and private sector entities. The project is funded by the U.S. Department of Commerce and managed by L.A. Trade and Baytrade.

TradePort helps U.S. businesses of all sizes and types to expand the market for their products throughout the world. For businesses new to exporting, TradePort offers interactive tutorial information to guide users through the transaction processes. Experienced exporters will find specific information to meet their advanced export information needs. The site includes an interactive trade tutorial, an extensive library of public and private databases, and a comprehensive search tool. More the 40,000 manufactures and service companies and hundreds of county and industry reports are available.

U.S. Small Business Administration

If you are a small business, the SBA will offer counseling and advice from international experts, training sessions and a variety of publications designed to assist smaller companies explore the potential of exporting. There are several programs available:

- *Export Information System (XIS):* An export/import database of trade information on 2,500 product categories.
- *Export Services Center (ESC):* Featured at the campuses of state universities; makes many of the university's resources available to the potential exporter.
- *Export Legal Assistance Network (ELAN):* Free legal advice for companies making their first entry into the export market.
- *Financial Assistance:* Programs include the Export Revolving Line of Credit, International Trade Loans, and co-sponsorship of Department of Commerce Matchmaker Trade Delegation Program participation.

Contact your local SBA office for more details.

State Department of Commerce

Each U.S. state has its own department of commerce or the equivalent, one of whose charters is to promote exports of locally produced goods and services. Some states are much more aggressive about this than others.

Your state may also have a group of export counselors who can help you with making export decisions, point you to information sources, or actually do research on your behalf.

Colleges and Universities

Some international business programs require field work or projects related to actual export situations. They may welcome your posing a research question from "real life" that students can then research for your and the students' benefit.

The American Graduate School of International Management, Glendale, AZ 85306, one of the top-rated international business schools, assigns such projects to small groups of students, who can turn out very valuable research. The school will request a modest stipend to cover the students' out-of-pocket costs. Contact Professor Shoshona Tancer at +1-602-263-2860.

Other institutions have similar programs.

FIELD WORK—SOURCES

Homebound research can take you only so far. There is no substitute for getting on an airplane and going there.

Trade Shows

Go to computer and software trade shows in the territory of interest. User group meetings are often also open to the public, and may be very informative. Do not neglect shows held in the United States. The large ones, and those billed as international, often attract a significant foreign attendance.

Trade Pubs

Most countries have national language computer trade publications. These are easier to find when you are in-country than from home. Do not neglect the homely telephone directory beside your hotel bed. It could be a gold mine.

Hardware Vendors

Do not neglect to contact the local hardware vendor organization in-country for the same help you requested at home. They will probably be able to be even more helpful.

Consultants

The consultant you employ to help you develop your overseas channels may well be foreign-based. Look for candidates when you travel abroad. Meet and interview interesting ones, including those you may have contacted when doing your homework. See the listing in the preceding Homework—Sources section.

Potential Distributors/Agents

Ask each potential channel partner you meet to name her major competitors, and the other strong players in her market. You will soon know much about the lay of the land in the country of interest. Remember, foreign country software markets are relatively small ponds compared to the United States. The real players all know each other.

Potential Customers

Try to meet possible customers of your product, and ask them from whom they would buy such products, and with whom they would recommend talking. Also, how valuable would they consider your product for their own use? Do a little prospecting. You can meet potential customers at trade shows of all kinds.

U.S. DOC Trade Missions

The U.S. Department of Commerce (DOC) sponsors trade missions all over the world. The sole purpose of these missions is to help U.S. exporters (or would-be exporters) to find suitable distribution or joint venture partners. The DOC arranges for all transportation, and its personnel accompanies each mission. If you participate, you can count on meeting a reasonably large number of potential partners. Some missions are specifically focused on software distribution. Contact the DOC for the current schedule, and to be placed on their mailing list.

U.S. DOC Distributor Search

One of the best bargains available to U.S. companies is the Department of Commerce Agent/Distributor search. For a very modest fee (<U.S. $100 per country), the DOC will, through the local embassy commercial staff, conduct a search of suitable partners. This will be a serious search, with several to a dozen companies identified that meet your prespecified profile. While the quality of the search may not be as high as if it were conducted by an industry specialist (the embassy personnel are generalists), the value is unbeatable. Even if you do not settle on one of the search result companies, they can be the start of a networking research project that should quickly acquaint you with the local market and its distribution possibilities.

Gold Key Visit

A kind of deluxe version of the above is the Gold Key visit. Here, the DOC will arrange for you and your colleagues a special tour of the geographical area of interest, complete with appropriate introductions. More expensive, but worthwhile to consider.

U.S. Embassies

Most U.S. embassies have a commercial section, with sector specialists, a library, and some research facilities. Especially if you give them advance notice, a visit the first time you arrive in a country is worthwhile. The staff will be very helpful, and can help answer questions about the local marketplace.

State Foreign Trade Offices

Many states have foreign field offices to help make local introductions, and to offer you the temporary use of a desk, phone, and receptionist while you are in the early stages of developing that market, all provided you are in the business of exporting products produced in that state.

DEMOGRAPHICS

Estimating the Size of Each Country Market

Determining the number of potential customers in a country is not necessarily easy. If your system software, for example, supports a certain operating system running on certain hardware platforms, then your market potential is approximately the installed base of the target environment. From this, you may need to subtract your competitors' installed base, unless you believe you can achieve replacement sales.

Often in the case of application products, the software will drive the hardware and system software selection of the customer. In that case, you need to know how many practitioners of the application discipline there are in the country. If your product is industry-specific, then obviously you will be interested in the size, competitiveness, and growth patterns of that industry in the country. These analyses are of exactly the same nature as those used for estimating domestic market size. However, the numbers may be more difficult to obtain.

Potential distributors, VARs, and customers in a target territory, if they are active in the market of interest, are very likely to have the market size information you seek, and will most often be willing to share it with you. Because of the rapidly changing nature of the computer industry, you will frequently be tracking a moving target. In some cases, you may be developing product to sell in a market that does not yet exist or is not yet mature. In these cases, market characteristics including distribution methods and sizing are more a matter of prediction than surveying.

The most important objective of market sizing is to be able to prioritize your country markets so that you can concentrate your earliest and strongest efforts in your best potential markets. Precise market size numbers are needed for accurate revenue forecasting, but these simply may be unobtainable in a reasonable amount of time. Estimates of absolute market size can be notoriously unreliable. At the least, though, you need good relative numbers. When comparing numbers, be sure they were obtained in the same manner, so that they will be consistent.

From the information you obtain, create a list of all potential country markets and their size in ranked order. Continue to update the list as you obtain further information and as markets change.

Table 3.3 is adapted from IDC data on the world computer market.

Other Critical Characteristics

If your products run on only certain models of hardware, or on certain levels or releases of operating systems, the populations of

Table 3.3. The World Computer Market

Country	Multiuser	Single User	Total	Percent
U.S.	27,415	70,450	97,865	37.5%
Japan	28,262	23,536	51,798	19.8%
Germany	5,879	11,516	17,395	6.7%
U.K.	4,390	7,136	11,526	4.4%
France	3,734	6,346	10,080	3.9%
Nordic	1,609	5,634	7,243	2.8%
Republic of Korea	1,066	5,388	6,454	2.5%
Canada	1,395	4,359	5,754	2.2%
Benelux	1,717	3,803	5,520	2.1%
Italy	2,536	2,755	5,291	2.0%
Australia	1,152	3,467	4,619	1.8%
China	597	3,225	3,822	1.5%
Brazil	1,242	2,418	3,660	1.4%
Switzerland	994	2,210	3,204	1.2%
Spain	998	1,697	2,695	1.0%
Rest of the World	6,102	18,099	24,201	9.3%
Total	89,088	172,039	261,127	100.0%

Note: 1995 figures given in U.S. millions of dollars.
Source: Adapted from Worldwide Information Technology Market (1996).
International Data Corporation, Framingham, MA.

those environments should be explored. In Japan, for example, a conservative customer base will often keep running an old but proven operating system (OS) release long after the vendor has dropped support for it in the rest of the world. If your product does not run on that flavor of OS, you will forego a significant part of the Japanese market.

In other countries, software buying decisions are inordinately influenced by certain third parties. In Korea and Taiwan, for example, IBM still has an unusually strong influence on the acquisition of third-party software, especially system software. If IBM has a strong alliance with one of your competitors in those countries, you may have a difficult time there.

In other countries, certain customers act as bellwethers for the whole marketplace. The state-owned oil company complex PDVSA in Venezuela is an example. Sell your products there, and the entire country will be more receptive to them.

Breakdown by Geography

The internal geographic distribution within a country can influence your distribution strategy there, and can even determine whether you attack that market now or later. France has a highly centralized information technology (IT) user base—it is mostly in Ile de France, the area containing Paris. In Brazil, a huge country geographically, most of the computers are found in São Paulo State, Rio de Janeiro State, and the small southern tip of the country.

Germany, on the other hand, is decentralized in this regard. Munich is the center of research and engineering computing; Frankfurt hosts many corporate headquarters and is the transportation hub; Düsseldorf is the financial center; Hamburg is the gateway to northern Germany and Scandinavia; the Ruhr is the industrial heartland; while Bonn at this writing shares with Berlin the status of national capital and home to government users. All are important IT markets, and to miss any would be to curtail your potential success in this major country market. Furthermore, it would be difficult, for example, for a Bavarian to sell effectively in the north of Germany, given the different dialects and regional cultures. The inverse is also true.

Implications to Distribution Strategy

Different distribution strategies are called for in different geographically distributed market types. You can sell directly in France from a Paris base, and be efficient. The same is not true in Germany from any single location. Eventually, to truly cover the market, you will have to establish at least three offices in that country.

TIMING AND TRENDS

Do Not Rush It

The overall pace of doing business internationally is generally acknowledged to be slower than in the United States. Travel is more

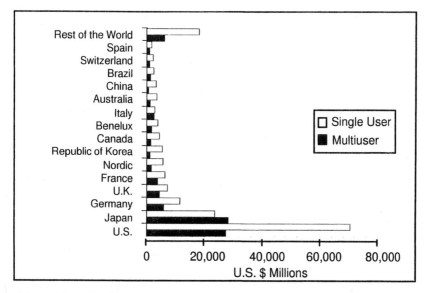

Adapted from Worldwide Information Technology Market (1995). International
Data Corp., Framingham, Massachusetts.

difficult and time-consuming, adding delays to meetings, while time
is needed to bridge both the business and cultural gaps between
would-be partners. Although the appeal of addressing a virgin market is strong, excessive haste in choosing the right channels in a
territory could easily lead to a mistake. Such a mistake might not
become evident for a year or more, and might take another year to
correct, given that alternatives would have to be found and launched.
Therefore, when making the critical decisions in choosing overseas
partners, meeting predetermined timetables should generally be
considered secondary to taking the time to make quality decisions.
In essence, nothing in an indirect sales situation is as important as
selecting effective distribution partners.

Nevertheless, to be realistic, your plan should acknowledge the
probable necessity of replacing established channel partners over
time.

Also, experience has shown that making the first few sales in a
country can be especially time-consuming. Initially there is no credibility for a product in a country, and many prospects do not want to

be the first to buy. Allow time between the signing of a new distribution partner and the first sale; the time allowance will likely vary in practice from one to nine months, or longer if translation or conversion is involved.

Maturity of Market

Will you lead or follow? As with any market, different strategies are called for depending upon whether you are early or late in the market. If you are first to market, you will probably have to convince customers that they need your product. If you are already successful in another country, this should not be exceptionally difficult.

If, on the other hand, you are entering a fully-penetrated market, then a replacement strategy is called for. Your focus will be on price, feature improvements, and service. None of these issues is novel in international sales. The novelty in global selling is that you may be the first to market in some geographies while facing penetrated markets in others, depending on what priorities your competitors have chosen. The caution is to not rigidly employ the same sales strategy everywhere without first examining critically the state of each market you enter.

Chapter 4

Market Entry Strategy

Markets dictate strategy. Strategy dictates organization.

—William Fath

DOING BUSINESS SUCCESSFULLY IN FOREIGN CULTURES

Our Cultural Assumptions and Biases

The United States is the most powerful and influential nation on earth. Many other countries have been capable of making that same boast during the ages of their ascendancies: China, Egypt, Greece, Italy (Rome), Spain, France, and England, among others. Citizens of those countries are proud of their nations' past glories and achievements. To ignore this pride or to belittle the importance of any country in the world is "geopolitically incorrect."

Yet the cultural "sea" that exists in the United States (as well as many other first-world countries) subtly positions the nationals of other counties as slightly less clever, less capable, less "human." These cultural biases are seen nowhere more clearly than on the nightly news. Local and national stories take precedence over all foreign events unless they are absolutely horrific in nature or happen to involve U.S. nationals. An earthquake in China that kills 4,000 is given less coverage than the kidnapping of a single American child. Furthermore, anything good that happens to the home country, even at the expense of any other, is given subtle praise. This kind of bias reflects the national culture, in jokes, ethnic characterizations, value decisions, and prejudices.

To be truly successful in international business, you must be able to first recognize this ethnocentricity, or nationalism. This is most easily done by making an effort to look at viewpoints and events through the eyes of another country's citizens. Then take care to express yourself in a culturally neutral context.

How to Talk

Idiomatic Speech

> The old geezer was meaner than a junkyard dog. He went the whole nine yards to bring home the bacon. Though we all thought it would be a slam-dunk, he nearly gave up the ghost trying to get the order.

How easy do you think it would be for a nonnative speaker of English who had never visited the United States to decode the previous paragraph? A good rule (of thumb?) is to cleanse your speech completely of idioms and other colorful figures if you want to be fully understood by foreigners (even by those who have English as their mother tongue, but are not from the United States and do not share your culture).

Language

It is best, of course, to converse fluently with people in their own language. This is an important goal, and anyone serious about international business should always be studying a foreign language. When in a country, try to pick up the language phrase by phrase. Do not be shy to ask your companions how to say, for example, "pass the salt, please," in their language. Say it aloud a few times, then use it again when you next want the salt.

When at home, work with language study tapes in the car on the way to the office. When traveling, use them on the airplane. Do not just listen, but repeat back aloud, answer the questions, participate as fully as possible.

It is true that English is the international language of business, especially in the field of software. But a lot of business is conducted in other languages, too. Certainly nationals of the same country do business with each other in the language of that country.

An American manager was once invited to sit in on a staff meeting of a Danish company, taking place in Germany. In attendance were the regional managers from France, Denmark, the Netherlands, and Spain. At the end of the meeting, the American thanked his host for conducting the meeting in English. He was surprised when the host replied that they always conducted these meetings in English, even though English was not the mother tongue of any of the attendees.

Nevertheless, learning at least a little of the local language, and having the courage to use it, albeit clumsily, will win you kudos from your hosts. As a rule, your channel partners will speak English, as will their commercial customers in Northern Europe and all former English colonies. Unless you speak the language, you will find it more difficult to make customer sales calls with your channel partners in Japan, Southern Europe (including France), and Latin America.

How to Relate

> To be a successful soldier, you must know history. What you must know is how man reacts.
>
> —*George S. Patton*

History

It may take years to learn a language fluently, but it takes only a few hours to learn the basic history of a country. Knowing the history of your host will help you to understand the people and how they are likely to feel about other nationals, and will give you a common topic of conversation.

The United States has only 220 years of history as a nation. Japan's culture is over 1,000 years old. Most European nations' histories also extend back more than a millennium or two.

How to Negotiate

Negotiation is key to business success abroad as well as at home. From the initial distribution agreement to setting next year's sales target, negotiation separates winners from losers in the global trading game.

Moreover, being a good negotiator at home does not guarantee the same success abroad. Americans, for example, typically have quite different negotiating styles than do the Swiss, the Japanese, or the Venezuelans. Knowing and appreciating these various styles may spell the difference between reaching productive agreements and leaving confused, frustrated, or angry would-be partners behind at the end of a business trip.

Frank Acuff, in his book, *How to Negotiate Anything with Anyone Anywhere Around the World,* describes the seven sins of the typical American negotiator:

1. Falling into the win-lose trap
2. Ignoring cultural gaps
3. Failing to recognize the host country's negotiating obstacles
4. Being in too much of a hurry
5. Not listening for communications barriers
6. Wearing blinders with respect to relationships and emotions
7. Using language that is too hard to understand

Acuff provides an excellent guide to negotiating abroad, including helping to recognize how negotiator counterparts from various cultures typically view each other, and how to optimize your negotiating strategy for each country.

Getting to Know You

Read international publications. This will give you a general awareness of conditions affecting various country markets, and may give you something intelligent to talk about over dinner.

There are a number of truly excellent periodicals with global scope, available on a subscription basis anywhere in the world:

International Herald Tribune (daily newspaper)
—A joint venture of *The New York Times* and *The Washington Post,* printed in several worldwide locations simultaneously. Short, immensely readable, very well written—a personal favorite, with a good international business section.

What's Working for American Companies in International Sales and Marketing
Progressive Business Publications
370 Technology Dr.
Malvern, PA 19355

telephone: +1-800-220-5000
fax: +1-610-647-8089

—A pricey bimonthly with lots of good, practical ideas on international marketing.

The Economist (monthly magazine)
—The classic on world business; erudite.

Regional ***Wall Street Journal*** (European, Asian, etc.; daily newspapers)

Financial Times (United Kingdom; daily newspaper)

Context and Communication

Attitudes toward time vary in different societies. Anthropologist Edward T. Hall's research found that time is not an absolute, but that, like space, it is culturally variable and programmed. In *Understanding Cultural Differences*, he goes on to define "high context" and "low context" cultures. In a high context culture, who you are matters a great deal; relationships matter; affiliations matter. Time is not a dominant value. In the opposite, a low context society, it is the transaction that counts, time is money, and business can be successfully conducted long distance over the telephone by people who will never meet.

According to Hall, low context cultures include those of the United States, Germany, Switzerland, Holland, the United Kingdom, and Scandinavia; most of the rest of the world is, to a greater or lesser extent, high context. He offers rules for citizens of one context orientation when dealing with those of the other. For low context individuals negotiating with high context people:

- *Manners*. Know their intricate rules of good manners: proper greetings, accepted personal distance, who goes first through a doorway, etc.

- *Time*. Slow down. Everything will take longer, so relax.
- *Meetings*. Expect meetings to flow of their own accord. Agendas will not exist, side meetings will occur.
- *Small talk*. Know the history and favorite sports so you have something to say.
- *Face*. Do not dominate. Do not show up your counterpart. Let her suggest the solution.

National Biases

Unfortunately, a long history has given nations many opportunities to conquer and oppress each other. As Jacques Delors, one of the key figures in the European Union, once said to a visitor from Canada, "In Canada you have too much space and too little history. In Europe, our problem is too little space and too much history."

Thus, many Serbs regard Bosnian Muslims with a murderous passion, owing to a chain of barbarity that began some 500 years ago when some members of the Christian Serbian nation sided with their Moslem Turkish conquerors.

Do not expect a German salesman to have much success in the Netherlands: the Dutch remember that the Nazis bombed Rotterdam to rubble at the outset of World War II as an object lesson. The lesson has not been forgotten.

Nor do Chinese and Koreans remember fondly their experiences with Japanese invaders during the same era. Some are not likely to relate well to Japanese businessmen.

A Dutch sales representative may not do too well in Belgium, even though the Flemings of northern Belgium speak the same language as the Dutch. Until 1830, what is now Belgium was part of the Netherlands, and the Catholic Belgians were oppressed by the Protestant Dutch.

Know also that the Norwegians like the Danes, because they were once part of the same country. But they stereotypically dislike the Swedes, with whom they were forcibly united in 1814.

These stereotypes of course have many exceptions among enlightened individuals. But in general, they are true enough of the time to provide a caution in setting up international distribution channels.

SELECTING PARTNERS

The Partner Profile

Very helpful in selecting channel partners is to compare their profiles with the profile of the model distributor that you have previously developed. The following is a model distributor checklist, more or less in order of importance:

- Experienced in the market of interest; successfully resells related products into the target market—but does not carry competitive products, or products whose path of development will likely take them into competition with your current or planned offerings.
- Willing to dedicate sufficient technical and sales resources, and to make that commitment in writing.
- Able to provide a credible and satisfactory two-year marketing plan for your products.
- Strong technical knowledge in your product area.
- Financially sound—strong balance sheet, minimum debt, liquid assets available to invest adequately in the new product line.
- Some years of history as a successful, profitable company. Using a startup or loss-generating firm is more risky. An exception might be a new company built around a very strong salesperson with particular abilities in your product area, well known in the territory marketplace.
- Good customer base—large, active list of current customers who will make viable prospects for your product.
- Good reputation with customers. Insist on directly checking references from at least half a dozen customers you choose at random from the distributor's customer list. Hire a native speaker if necessary to conduct the poll.
- No significant conflict with your interests in the ownership of the company. A large minority shareholder, for example, who also controls a distributor of competitive products would be cause for concern.

- Not representing so many products that yours will get lost. If the company does represent many products, this problem can successfully be solved by having your product handled by a focused division or group within the distributor organization.
- Good credit history. Check Dun and Bradstreet (your law firm or accountant may have a subscription if you do not), which researches firms worldwide.
- Good "chemistry" with you and your colleagues. Dynamic, energetic, growth-oriented. Compatible business cultures, given the differences in territory culture.
- Nonlitigious—no history of suing vendors, customers, et al.
- Willing to buy initial stocking inventory, or prepay some royalties. This may or may not be a realistic expectation depending on how hot a product you have to offer.

Fath offers another form of distributor checklist on page 75 of *How to Develop and Manage Successful Distributor Channels in World Markets.*

First Contact

You may wish to correspond initially with a potential partner via letter (faxed or e-mailed), something to the effect of the following:

> Dear XXX,
>
> Our firm, Vendor, Inc., develops and sells ＿＿＿ products for the ＿＿＿ industry. Our sales last year exceeded U.S. $＿＿＿. Our product ＿＿＿ was rated among the top ＿＿＿ of its type last year by ＿＿＿. We have over ＿＿＿ customers in ＿＿＿ countries. The company was founded in ＿＿＿.
>
> We are now looking at further international expansion in (XXX's country or region), and would like to discuss the possibility of a distribution partnership with you. I would enjoy hearing from you about this subject. Please contact me at ＿＿＿＿＿＿ (fax, telephone, or e-mail address).
>
> Best regards,

Attachments could include:

- product brochures
- price list
- corporate brochure
- white paper on product direction and strategy

Maggiori's *How to Make the World Your Market* also contains an excellent example of such a letter.

The Territory Marketing Plan

After the distribution agreement is executed, partner sales and technical training will take place. The marketing plan as developed by the new channel partner will be reworked with your input as required, and the desired positioning of the products will be determined by the partner in consultation with your marketing staff.

Customization of the products will begin, including user manuals, training materials, and marketing collateral. This will include language translation as needed.

In addition to technical support, and probably more important, is marketing support and consulting to the partner. Partners are most productive when they are supported effectively and communicated with often. Frequent visits will help keep a significant mindshare. Periodic meetings will aid in communication and help build enthusiasm.

A channel partner should be treated as a blend between a customer and a branch sales office. A win-win relationship will be fostered with a long-term mentality, assuming consistent performance. Visibility into the partner's outlook will be obtained by review of a marketing plan from each partner, updated annually.

You will be assisting your partners in determining how best to position the products in light of the current local perceptions and prejudices of the marketplace. You will advise on communicating that positioning to the local trade press, opinion leaders, and marketplace in general. Marketing support will be an ongoing need by your partners.

Territory Marketing

The channel partner will begin marketing in the territory as soon as possible after the training and the marketing plan have been completed. The marketing program will typically include seminars, publicity, direct mail, and advertising, where appropriate.

Creating the appropriate publicity about your international activities is vital. Opening a new distribution relationship or especially a subsidiary in a country can be news there. A good multinational public relations firm will provide a worldwide press release program. The PR firm can customize product and general company releases for each country market, place them in appropriate trade publications, and follow up by telephone with editorial staffs. This approach to central release distribution will promote uniformity and timeliness worldwide on releasing information. The costs may be shared with the channel, as part of their territory marketing function is being performed centrally.

Participate in selected international trade shows in support of the distributors. Participation in such major shows lends credibility to your products and provides visibility of competitive and market trends. The leading shows in Europe for software are Systems in Munich and CeBIT in Hannover, Germany. The latter, a multi-tracked general computer show, is the world's largest, with some 600,000 attendees. The former is more focused on software.

NEGOTIATING THE AGREEMENT

In all territories, potential partners, once interested in representing the company, should be thoroughly investigated as described above as well as for the characteristics listed in the Partner Profile.

Preparing Model Contracts

The form of distributor agreement embodies the whole structural nature of the relationship with your foreign partner. It details what part of the revenues come to you and what part the partner keeps, and what the obligations are to each partner for marketing, sales, conversion, translation, pre- and post-sales support, billing, and collection.

There is a sample software distribution agreement included in Appendix 3. See also Fath's *How to Develop and Manage Successful Distributor Channels in World Markets* for a checklist of items to be included in the agreement, as well as other contract pointers for international distribution.

Having standard model contracts on the shelf will save a lot of time up front and in the future. Creating contracts from scratch or using the last fully negotiated one as a baseline will lead to endless confusion.

The Business Proposition

The distribution agreement, most importantly, *must reflect a business proposition that will make money for both you and your partner.* There is no use in being such a shrewd and hard-headed negotiator that you get all the contract points in your favor. If you get a huge royalty split (or tiny discount), and have no responsibilities other than to deliver product, the partner may grudgingly sign up if it is the best deal to be had. But there will not be the level of investment (to say nothing of enthusiasm) in the marketplace needed to optimize penetration and coverage for your product. It is better to be a little generous with contract terms, especially at first. You will end up getting a slightly smaller piece of a much bigger pie. It will start the relationship off with good feelings and optimism on the part of the partner, and nothing is more critical.

The revenue split between your firm and your partner need not be fixed forever. It may well be advisable to take a smaller split for the first year, when investment of the partner will be higher, and revenues lower. This approach could result in a faster liftoff for your products in the territory. The important thing is to make sure that both you and your partner can profit from the deal.

Conversely, once the product is established, you want the partner to maximize revenues every year, and not hold back on closing (or worse, reporting) some deals until the next quota period. An approach to solving this problem is to establish a sliding royalty (or discount) scale so that, for example, those sales made over quota will gain the partner a better split each year than those made before meeting quota.

Keeping Options Open

Negotiations with at least two potential qualified channel partners in each country should be entered into simultaneously so as to promote competition for the product line and produce the most advantageous contract terms. Each of the finalists should be requested to develop a two-year marketing plan for the products. Up-front consideration, credited against future expense reimbursements and royalty payments, might be necessary to help encourage the partner to make the required marketing investment in a timely manner.

Effective Use of Third Parties

Sometimes having an intermediary aid you in negotiating partner agreements can be helpful. If you employed a consultant to help you locate candidate partners, this firm may be also qualified to begin negotiation for you and to accompany and advise you during the entire process.

The United States is the most litigious country, and tends to have more complex legal agreements than those commonly found in other lands. Foreign distribution firms may take offense at the intense legalese found in a typical U.S. distribution contract (including the one in Appendix 3 of this book!), which attempts to spell out every conceivable contingency and catalogs a complete litany of possible faults you might find in the performance of your potential partner. Such drafts imply very little mutual trust. Foreign agreements of this kind are, on the other hand, usually much shorter, more general, and speak to the intent rather than the detailed mechanics of the proposed relationship.

But experienced partners know that to do business with U.S. firms, a complex agreement is often the price of entry. In most cases, it is neither necessary nor advisable to get lawyers directly involved in the negotiation. This could tend to get your prospective foreign partner very nervous.

Your counsel absolutely should review any drafts prior to execution, and advise you off-line on the legal implications of each proposed term and condition. But unless you get hopelessly bogged down in legal, rather than purely business issues, the lawyer does not need to be at the negotiating table.

When negotiating an agreement with a German distributor which was a subsidiary of a major German manufacturer, a U.S. software firm asked for a financial guarantee from the parent (recommended standard practice). The parent balked. After a lot of fruitless indirect communication with respective counsel, the American firm finally had to get its U.S.-based German lawyer talking directly to the distributor's lawyer in Germany. Between them they came up with a "Patronatserklärung," a strictly German legal device which accomplished what was asked for, within legal parameters that the German partners felt comfortable with.

The Negotiation Process

The process of negotiating the partnership agreement (be it a distributorship, a VAR, a joint venture) will help each of you to determine and define exactly how the relationship is to work in practice. Will sales forecasts be required, and if so, when are they due? How long after a sale is payment due? In what currency? At what conversion rate? And so forth. Do not rush the process. It is very useful, and can lay the groundwork for a surprise-free relationship.

The way the contract is actually negotiated will tell you something about your potential partner. A tough, businesslike negotiator is good. If the negotiation is too easy or too difficult, maybe you have not chosen the best match. Do not feel compelled to complete every deal. If you took the advice given above, you have at least one, and perhaps two alternate partners waiting in the wings, to whom you have not said "no" yet, and to whom you can now take your agreement.

An important part of the contract negotiation process is getting a preview of how the relationship is likely to work out. The negotiation will, you hope, be the most contentious and stressful part of the entire relationship. If the process remains friendly and efficient, that bodes well for the relationship. Do not rule out terminating negotiations if you find the people across the table too difficult to deal with, even if you are getting your way with the contract.

Local versus Domestic Counsel

You will already have corporate counsel, external, and perhaps internal as well. Existing counsel may be equipped to do an adequate job of helping you in setting up international operations. But that is not likely to be the case in every country of interest. Knowledge of local law and practice is essential in entering into an agreement regarding doing business in any country. Table 4.1 presents some sources for international corporate counsel.

Table 4.1. Lawyers Around the World

Baker & McKenzie, the world's largest law firm, has branches around the United States and affiliated firms in virtually every major international market. Counsel located in your nearest branch office can coordinate all foreign legal contacts and allow you to deal with only one person. Contact headquarters at:

Baker & McKenzie
First Prudential Plaza
130 East Randolph Drive, Suite 3500
Chicago IL 60601

telephone: +1-312-861-8000
fax: +1-312-861-2898
fax: +1-312-861-2899

Alternatively, you may prefer to select and interact with local in-country counsel on your own. Here are some ways to find good local firms:

Interlaw is an international association of forty-eight independent law firms covering more than seventy-five key commercial centers in Europe, North and South America, and Asia Pacific. Members are high-quality firms with an emphasis on international activity. Contact:

Interlaw Secretariat
3600 Two Allen Center
1200 Smith St.
Houston, TX 77002

telephone: +1-703-951-5838
fax: +1-703-653-1871
e-mail: lbecker@bpl.com

Commercial Law Affiliates is a network of over 185 firms with offices in some 200 cities covering more than sixty-eight countries. The network employs a worldwide client satisfaction measurement system and formal information sharing among its attorneys.

Commercial Law Affiliates
420 N. Fifth St.
Suite 970
Minneapolis, MN 55401

telephone: +1-612-339-8680
fax: +1-612-337-5783
e-mail: cclaxcom@counsel.com

Pacific Rim Advisory Counsel is an alliance of over twenty-five major independent law firms covering Argentina, Australia, Brazil, Hong Kong, India, Indonesia, Japan, Korea, Malaysia, Mexico, New Zealand, Philippines, Singapore, South Africa, Taiwan, Thailand, and the United States. Contact:

Hogan & Hartson L.L.P.
8300 Greensboro Dr.
McLean, VA 22102

telephone: +1-703-848-2600
fax: +1-703-448-7650

The Alliance of European Lawyers has offices in Belgium, the Netherlands, France, Poland, Sweden, Germany, Spain, the United Kingdom, the Czech Republic, and the United States. U.S. address:

Alliance of European Lawyers
712 Fifth Ave.
30th Floor
New York, NY 10019

telephone: +1-212-801-3400
fax: +1-212-801-3405

Other Networks
Listings of other legal networks may be found in the *Martindale-Hubbell* domestic and international legal directories.

Audit and Accountability

Doing business with channel partners many thousands of miles distant carries the inherent risks of fraud and dishonesty. It is easier in this situation to envision sales made and not reported, incorrect reporting of prices, and other deceitful practices than for a domestic sales force. Although these activities cannot be precluded with 100 percent certainty, the following steps, at a minimum, can be taken with all channel partners:

- careful reference checking prior to entering into a business arrangement;
- frequent visits to the channel partner and its customers;
- attendance and intelligence gathering at international trade shows where customers would be likely to attend;
- annual submission of certified financial reports;
- formal periodic audits, both by the partner's auditors and by a local firm retained by your company.

Risk will be minimized working with only established, reputable companies.

Revenue Recognition

Normally, revenue from distributors is recognized upon execution of the end-user contract. Revenue recognized equals the company's portion of the total revenue. Maintenance revenue is recognized ratably over the maintenance period. When applicable, the exchange rate on the date that revenue is recognized will be used, both for recording of revenue and for payment by the distributor.

There is also an option, used by a few U.S. software companies, of recognizing the entire end-user contract value as revenue, and recording the distributor's share as an expense. This can be done with a true distributor, but may require your countersignature on the end-user contract.

Obviously, this latter method will show larger revenues and smaller profit margins.

Receivables and Cash Flow

A major topic of negotiation might be payment terms. This is sensitive to a channel partner, because few of these are cash-rich businesses, and few are in a position to front a lot of money.

Typically, the partner will not want to pay you before he is paid. You might insist on his buying stocking inventories if your position in the market is strong. Otherwise, try to arrange payment to you within the same month that the partner receives his cash.

The problem with stating such a term in the agreement is that it is difficult to audit or enforce. You generally will not know when the partner receives payment, and thus cannot accurately do dunning or receivables aging. What you will know is when the product subli-cense is sold. Thus the negotiation may revolve around how long an end user in the territory usually takes to pay.

In Northern Europe, this is often thirty days. In Southern Europe, it may be much longer. Italian companies routinely take 120 to 180 days to pay invoices. The Italian government routinely takes one year. Spain is nearly as bad. This occurs despite the vendor (your partner) having to pay a value-added tax on the transaction within about a month of the sale. Consulting with your Big 6 accounting partner and your colleagues in other software firms will help you add some reality to this discussion.

Getting Paid

Not receiving payment for a single transaction is rare in software export, and seldom too costly. Far more dangerous are situations where a distribution partner owes you a lot of money for many sales, and will not or cannot pay. "Will not pay" usually implies a dispute, which you need to resolve, probably face-to-face, and with luck and skill, not in front of a judge or arbitration panel. This section is more directed to the "cannot pay" scenario.

It is unusual but not unknown for a distribution partner to lose or spend your share of sales on other things, such as promoting other products in its line that look more attractive at the moment; meeting debt calls on failed real-estate transactions, or having the money embezzled by a dishonest employee (the author has had personal experience with each). Or through poor management the company may simply go bankrupt, and be placed in receivership. You may find yourself an unsecured creditor in line with many others, none of whom will be paid at anything like parity. How do you protect yourself?

Of course, none of these contingencies is limited to software export. They can happen in any credit business right at home. But it is often harder to see them coming from a distance. The cardinal rule is, do not let the debt get too large or too old. *Establish a maximum line of credit with each partner, manage it, and enforce it.* Have fixed, written procedures in place that spell out what you do in case the credit line is exceeded. You may withhold shipment, issue a warning letter of default, or get on a plane.

Letter of Credit

The classical mechanism for exporters to assure that they are paid for their goods is the irrevocable letter of credit (LOC). The LOC is issued by the importer's bank to a correspondent bank in the exporter's country. It guarantees payment to the exporter's account when certain very specific conditions have been met and properly documented.

Typically, documents evidencing title to the goods must be delivered to the importer's bank to trigger payment under the LOC. The freight forwarder will deliver the relevant documents to the exporter, who then submits them to the correspondent bank. The bank approves them if they are in good order and forwards the documents to the importer's bank. If there are no discrepancies, the importer's bank transfers funds to the exporter's account and releases the documents to the importer, allowing him to clear the goods through customs and take legal possession.

Rules governing these transactions are established uniformly by UCP 500 (Uniform Customs and Practice for Documentary Credits, 1993 revision, International Chamber of Commerce Publication 500), rather than a myriad of national jurisdictions. See Fath's *How to Develop and Manage Successful Distributor Channels in World Markets* for a more complete description of LOCs and their many variants.

This approach works well for many exporters of tangible goods. In practice in the software industry, however, the LOC had proven cumbersome and unnecessary when dealing with all but the most uncreditworthy of importers. There is negligible cost of manufacturing in software, and the loss due to nonpayment is likely to be limited to a few transactions. It is unlikely in most cases that this will have a material financial effect on the exporter. More practical approaches are described below.

Guarantee by the Parent Company

The simple precaution you can take when dealing with any subsidiary company is to insist on a financial guarantee from its parent. This is especially relevant if the subsidiary is small in comparison to the parent. Any distribution agreement with a subsidiary should contain such a financial guarantee, signed off by the parent. You are well within custom to insist on such a clause, although the subject must be handled delicately with subsidiary management to avoid insult.

Security Interest

Another approach is obtaining a security interest in debt from your distribution partner or customer. This is a legal approach similar to a Uniform Commercial Code filing in the United States. In the case of bankruptcy or receivership, it may put you closer to the head of the line when remaining assets are divided up.

The problem is that not many countries include the concept of security interest as part of national law. Good local counsel is essential here.

Lock Box

In a problem situation where you entertain doubts about receiving your money, a lock box arrangement can be set up. A lock box is essentially a bank account to which customers send their payments. The money is disbursed automatically by the bank.

Say you have a 50/50 royalty arrangement with a distributor. You jointly set up the lock box account (or either of you may do this—it is a matter of trust and negotiation), then issue an irrevocable standing order to the bank, for example: "Disburse 50 percent of all receipts to each party's separate account daily." The distributor must agree that all invoices for your products to its customers specify the lock box as the payment address.

Customers need never know of this arrangement, as the payment instructions can read, for instance, "Please forward payment to Distributor XYZ, Box 123, etc.," which happens to be the bank's lock box. You get paid as soon as your distribution partner does.

One weakness of this arrangement is that it requires you to audit the distributor's invoices to make sure that the agreement is being kept. Also, most distributors will not be especially enthusiastic about this approach. Not only does it implicitly impugn their trustworthiness, it deprives them of the cash flow and float that such a business normally thrives on. But it can be effective.

Passwords, Time-Outs, and License Management

A very effective way to control the use of your products abroad, and thus increase the likelihood of your being paid for them, is the use of installation passwords. For products where such protection would not be considered necessary or even desirable in the United States or Canada, it may be highly desirable to you as well as acceptable to customers in jurisdictions that offer poor intellectual property protection. Mass-market PC products probably are not candidates for such protection, but higher-priced PC-hosted offerings as well as server- and mainframe-based products may be.

Temporary installation passwords give the distributor the chance to provide customer trials that may begin and end at unpredictable times. Expiring passwords can be used as a sales tool to help hasten a buy decision.

Passwords can be linked not only to the date, but the CPU identifier or serial number of the machine in larger installations, to prevent unauthorized transfers. However, this kind of restriction can get unwieldy in fast-changing distributed environments.

One recommended strategy is to provide distribution channel partners with *temporary password generators*. These can be small programs that run on a PC, and produce an installation password that enables the product for a selectable period. You might, for instance, provide temporary password generators that issue passwords for periods of up to thirty days, but for only the current calendar year. A new generator would then be sent out to each partner annually, providing that a valid distribution agreement is in force with that partner (and that the partner's account is current). This gives the channel the flexibility to respond to requirements to install product on a moment's notice, while still restricting access.

For permanent or longer-term passwords, application must be made directly to you (the product owner). This could be via an e-mail specifying the end-user name and address, and the type and quantity of products to be installed. A routine could be written to automatically respond with the password if the required information is entered and the channel partner is in good standing. The password checking routine embedded in the product would issue a console warning a number of weeks prior to actual expiration of any password.

In this way, you will not be at the mercy of a rogue distributor who continues copying, selling, and installing your software after the termination of the relationship. Using this approach, you should have a record of every customer, and can contact them to transfer the license to a new entity if and when the need arises.

In a distributed or client/server environment, the issue of license management becomes more complex. Do you permit the product to be installed on many computers, but limit the number of concurrent users? Do you manage licensing from a central server on the network? How do you handle site and corporate licensing? These are common pricing policy questions. Your chosen approach can be enforced by the use of available license management products. An example is FLEX lm™ from Globetrotter Software, Cupertino, California, USA.

Another approach is that of a hardware key, or dongle. A PC dongle is a device that plugs into a parallel port, and then replicates that port so that any parallel device can be plugged into it—thus not tying up the port. Within the dongle is some circuitry that is queried by the software product, which will not run unless the proper dongle is in place. Caution—in many countries, customers will not appreciate this kind of security. In others where it is most necessary they will tolerate it.

There are always tradeoffs with this kind of security. The product will be a bit more difficult to install, and may be less flexible in configuration. Legitimate customers may occasionally be inconvenienced. The channel will have to go through some otherwise unnecessary work. But many firms have found some kind of software security worthwhile in overseas markets.

The standard caveat applies: all security mechanisms are potentially breakable. A sufficiently determined hacker will be able, with enough time, to bypass password protection.

Prepayment

And, simplest of all, request payment prior to shipment. This may take the form of a prepaid royalty or prepaid stocking order. When good funds have been received (typically by wire transfer), ship the product.

Termination

Even though the sample distribution agreement contract in Appendix 3 contains at least six ways you can terminate the relationship, be aware that to make any termination smooth and productive, to avoid loss of sales momentum, to maintain the sales pipeline, and minimize adverse market fallout, you may need to be prepared to pay a significant sum (possibly out of future sales) to your former distribution partner to gain her cooperation.

SETTING UP YOUR OWN FOREIGN OPERATIONS

The major advantage of having your own operations in foreign markets is control. You may have a great distribution network in a particular country one year, with low investment on your part and high margins. The next year, the network may get caught up in a new, exciting product from another company, and your local sales start to tail off as attention and effort shift to the new product. Or your super distributor may undergo a reorganization or a key individual may resign, leaving you represented by a raw crew that once again needs your training and handholding. Even worse, you and the new manager may not get along, and personalities may interfere with business. These not uncommon eventualities can leave you with nothing you can do except perhaps cycle channel partners in the territory with expensive and disruptive consequences.

With your own operation, you can control what is sold, and how. The local entity can concentrate all its efforts on selling your company's products. Management is of your own choosing, and is strongly motivated to cultivate the relationship.

Ultimately, most mature software firms choose for these reasons to have owned operations in all major markets. Do not expect higher margins necessarily. Third-party channels can be very efficient. Do expect higher investment. Local operations are not casual commitments. Also expect much higher levels of management involvement on your part.

Setting strategies, policies and procedures, resolving disputes and difficulties, and dealing directly with local employment and contract issues will absorb management time and bandwidth. However, the rewards are commensurate. Revenue streams become more predictable. The benefits of marketing investments in the territory accrue to you alone. The revenue from high-margin maintenance contracts need not be shared.

How do you go about it?

Sources of Help

In addition to your legal counsel and your international accounting firm, there are some special sources of assistance to get you off to a good start.

Foreign Government Assistance

Contact the country's or region's government agency that assists foreign firms in setting up local operations. These can be found through the embassy or local consulate in your home country. Almost every country, and many subordinate geographies, have such agencies.

Their purpose is to bring trade and investment into their area. They will help with site selection, local introductions, tax and legal advice, and much more. And it is all free. Remember that all the world's economies compete for investment and jobs, so you are the prospective customer when dealing with these agencies. Let them wine and dine you if you are serious about investing in their locations.

American Chambers of Commerce

Virtually every country has an American Chamber of Commerce. These are organizations made up of expatriate American business people and representatives of U.S.-owned multinationals. (Remember, once you set up a foreign subsidiary, you will also be a multinational company.) The Chambers act as mutual self-help organizations and can assist you in establishing the network of contacts you will need to succeed in the territory. If you are a U.S. firm, encourage your local national manager to join.

Recruiting and Hiring Nationals

In *Selling Software in the Global Market, 1996-97,* Ken Lewis found from surveying software exporters that cultural differences, language, time zones, and physical distances were the most often-cited causes of difficulty in managing foreign channels. Of the respondents indicating that they were making changes in these areas, 85 percent specifically mentioned "hiring local, dedicated, or multilingual staff or management" (p. 13).

There is literally no substitute for knowledgeable, experienced native trading experts on the ground working to represent your products. Other approaches may work after a fashion, but they will not be optimal.

Compensation

Develop a compensation package before starting the recruiting process. A search firm or your Big 6 accountant can help you with this. Do not be surprised if in high-cost countries in Europe or Asia, the package completely blows away your domestic pay standards. Company cars are also a very common perk in many countries, if only for tax reasons. You may not have any company cars at home, but you will abroad. Do not let that stop you. You will have to play by local rules if you expect to attract the best.

One potent weapon the U.S. company has in the headhunting game is the stock option. These are rare abroad, but properly explained and promoted, can be very attractive to a foreign national, and may permit a reduction in other cash compensation elements.

Where to Find Them

Locating key nationals is critical to success. Here are five possible sources:

Your Channel Partners. The same sales manager who works for your distributor or VAR may make an excellent employee. No longer spread between multiple vendors' product lines and no longer subject to the potentially conflicting priorities of a third-party organization, this person can become very productive for you. She already knows your product and customers in the country.

If you plan to leave the nonexclusive partnership in place, approach the senior management of the firm first, and negotiate the right to recruit the individuals you want. You may agree to pay a recruiting fee, which likely the distributor had to pay itself at one time.

As part of your negotiation to terminate the partnership agreement (if exclusive), make sure you have the right to hire the staff. This will actually be an advantage to some European firms who may have long-term financial obligations by law to employees that they may no longer have need for without your products to sell.

Large International Recruiting Firms. Familiar names such as Korn/Ferry International, Heidrick & Struggles, and Robert Half have a strong international presence. These firms, though expensive, will generally do an excellent job for you. Make sure there is a software specialist on staff in the country you are interested in, and meet that person face-to-face before proceeding. Work out job descriptions and compensation carefully in advance.

Regional Firms. There are many good local and regional recruiting firms in each country. Your accountant, lawyer, or U.S. commercial attaché may be able to refer you. Some conduct full retainer searches; others will pass candidates to you, charging only if you hire.

Networking. Talk to your colleagues in other software firms. Go to trade shows in the country of interest, and meet the exhibitors. Ask to meet the local manager. Keep a database of everyone you meet in a country over time. Call them and ask them for referrals.

Do It Yourself. This is difficult unless you speak the local language, and have a place in-country to receive mail, telephone calls, and conduct interviews. Some U.S. states have foreign offices set up to aid state-resident exporters to penetrate certain markets. If your state has such an office, it may be able to be used for this purpose.

Expatriate Considerations

An alternative to hiring nationals is to transfer domestic employees.

High Cost

Relocating a domestic employee to a foreign country for a temporary assignment is expensive. Especially if a family is involved, count on a total cost to the company of two to three times the cost of employing the same individual at home. Expense considerations include the often higher cost of living in the new location, housing and car allowances, children's schooling, trips home, and moving costs. As tempting as it is to have on the ground in the new market a known, trusted person who thoroughly knows your business and products, the expatriate may lack certain other vital knowledge, such as the language and the local market. In the end, these factors, combined with the expense, will often promote the decision against long-term expatriate assignments.

Relocation

Moving to a foreign country can be a very disorienting experience. Even though the employee will be involved with a familiar business, it will be in an unfamiliar culture, and many aspects of life taken for granted at home will be different. This usually is not a severe problem for an unmarried person, but is magnified when a whole family moves abroad, especially for the first time.

The spouse and children must cope with a completely unfamiliar environment and will lack many of their accustomed support systems. It is estimated that nearly one-third of foreign temporary relocations of families fail, with the employee admitting defeat and requesting an immediate transfer home.

The chance of this eventuality can be reduced by prerelocation counseling of the employee and the family. Experienced professional counselors are available to help prepare family members for their new experience, and to equip them mentally to deal with the inevitable onset of culture shock.

Tax Treatment

The expatriate may very well become subject to foreign income taxes. For instance, though the U.S. Internal Revenue Service generally credits income taxes paid abroad against U.S. income tax liability, the foreign rate may be substantially higher.

There are a number of special legal considerations and techniques that may be used to minimize or avoid high expatriate taxes. For example, in many EU countries, if you spend less than 183 nights per tax year actually in the country, there will be no local income tax. If the employee has regional responsibility, and travels outside the country in the region, back to headquarters, and vacations abroad, it may be possible to slip under the 183-day rule. Or, if the one-year assignment begins in the middle of a tax year (not necessarily a calendar year), it may be possible spend 360 consecutive days in the country without tripping the 183-day rule.

These loopholes must be carefully researched and planned out in advance. Even so, the total tax burden on the expat may very likely be higher than if he stayed at home. In that case, you may agree to *gross up* the employee's wages, by adding the amount necessary to make the new net pay equal to the old net pay.

These calculations and other advice should be sought from an accounting firm with presence and knowledge in the country of interest as well as in the United States. As the employee is likely to have to complete two income tax returns, one of which will be totally unfamiliar, it is also common for the company to offer to have both returns prepared by the international accounting firm at the company's expense. You do not want the employee to have to spend a lot of time and attention on tax matters when there will be more important marketing and sales issues to attend to.

The Expatriate Agreement

A written agreement between the employee and the company, prepared and agreed to before the foreign assignment begins is most strongly recommended. It should cover all economic aspects of the assignment, such as:

- What is the assignment
- Duration of assignment
- Trips back home—for the employee, for the family—how often, who pays
- Salary uplift
- Compensation paid in what currency
- Company paid housing—how much
- Company paid legal expenses—visas, work permits
- Company paid income tax return preparation—local and home country

- Company paid children's schooling
- Job upon return
- Retirement, vacation, other benefit accruals
- How is local medical care paid

Tax and Legal Considerations

See Chapter 3 regarding tax and legal considerations of doing business abroad. When setting up foreign subsidiaries, you will be subject to local income tax. Many jurisdictions, both on the national and regional levels, offer favorable tax treatment to companies setting up new operations in their territories. Incentives are related to the amount of investment, the number of employees to be hired locally, and the relative poverty of the region selected. Such tax treatment should be sought in advance of selecting the final location for the establishment. Negotiation with one or more jurisdictions will tend to yield the most favorable outcome. With your local attorney, request a tax ruling from the jurisdiction prior to finally deciding on the location. You may get a multiyear tax holiday, or reduced rates for a period of time.

Timetable

The sample timetable shown in Table 4.2 is a possible checklist of steps you may need to accomplish in setting up your foreign subsidiary. The timing will vary widely by jurisdiction. You should establish your own timetable after conferring with counsel and other advisors. Use it as a roadmap within your organization to ensure all critical tasks are accomplished in a timely manner.

Communication

Communicating with your owned foreign operations is even more important than with your third-party channel partners. You are completely responsible, and completely at risk. Also, the potential rewards are higher. So you have to be closely involved with the planning and decision-making process and know quickly if something is not going right.

Table 4.2. Sample Timetable for Establishing
a New Foreign Subsidiary or Branch

Number of weeks *before* trading starts	Action
16	create pro forma first-year income statement including compensation structure
15	begin recruiting local manager
15	select local legal counsel
14	select entity structure
14	choose entity name
14	search entity name
12	begin entity registration process
10	begin search for premises
10	draft employment contracts
8	make offer to new manager
6	obtain copies of existing end-user license agreements in territory, if any
4	obtain VAT or company tax number
4	register for social security/withholding tax
4	new manager starts
4	open bank account
4	arrange for insurance
4	execute premises lease
4	arrange for bookkeeping or accounting
4	order furniture
4	order computers, software
3	begin recruiting additional staff
3	begin arrangements for press conference/open house
3	contract for/arrange for local payroll service
3	order telephones
3	print stationery/business cards
3	begin building customer/prospect database
1	arrange e-mail and answering service
0	trading begins

Number of weeks *after* trading starts	Action
1	send letters to existing customers announcing new entity
1	establish help line
1	send letters to existing customers (if any) requesting assignment of license agreements to new entity
1	hire additional staff
2	press conference/open house announcing new entity

At a minimum, establish a monthly reporting and sales forecasting regime. Scrutinize the monthly income statement, balance sheet and cash flows. Frequent telephone conversations with your local manager are also in order, no matter the time zone difference.

Also participate closely in the recruiting of key individuals—sales staff, technical manager. Make sure that you and your foreign office manager agree on position profiles and critical characteristics of successful candidates. The finalist should be interviewed by a senior home office executive before the final offer is made.

Communication with the subs and the branches involves at minimum several trips a year in each direction. Be sure to include appropriate foreign staff in headquarters' management meetings, sales kickoffs, quota clubs, and product training. Involve executives and managers from outside the international department in visits to foreign offices and international staff meetings. Marketing, domestic sales, development, and finance managers all need to know the foreign office managers. Valuable communication will flow both ways.

Sometimes the foreign operation needs a communications champion, a powerful spokesperson at the head office. Communications can go horribly wrong: critical technical questions do not get answered on time, and competitors win a big sale. Finance neglects to wire the rent money, and the landlord is ordering your staff out of its Paris office. It is time for you to step in and do whatever is necessary to ensure that that distant voice *does* get heard at headquarters.

If there is an internal newsletter, be sure the international field gets their share of mentions. They usually cannot attend the company picnic or the Christmas party to take advantage of the informal communication that such events foster. You will have to come up with substitutes.

In fact, raising the level of awareness of the foreign field staff at headquarters and around the corporation is a very important part of international management's job.

THE INTERNATIONAL BUSINESS PLAN

Having completed your research, and reached conclusions as to how international expansion should proceed, the next step is to create a business plan for international operations. Failing to do this will likely result in an approach that is chaotic, inefficient, and not well communicated to the rest of the organization. Without a plan, you will not be able to measure success or failure, and will have a difficult time seeing where you are and where you are going from day to day.

Going international is a major investment, and good business practice calls for a fairly detailed plan. The following is a possible structure. Another is given in Herman J. Maggiori's *How to Make the World Your Market*.

Model Business Plan Structure

Setting Goals and Objectives

Why is this being done? Indicate the reasons or goals expected from the successful execution of the plan. For example:

- Obtain 40 percent of company revenue from international within four years.
- Capture a faster-growing market.
- Spread development costs over a larger base.

Foreign sales may offset hard economic times at home. Often the economies of the English-speaking countries rise and fall roughly in concert, while the rest of the world follows a countercyclical pattern.

World Market for Our Products

Results of your demographic research.

Prioritization of Country Markets

Priorities and schedules for entering various geographies. Figure 4.1 summarizes a hypothetical plan for scheduling and prioritizing your marketing rollout in various territories, along with the cumulative worldwide share of the market you would be able to sell to after accomplishing each step of the plan. A graph is included to show this cumulative market coverage progression.

Overall unit sale projections by country for the first three years are estimated by using an average product price of U.S. $80,000. Worldwide penetration of 5 percent is realized at the end of three years, with 5 percent to 6 percent being achieved in the major countries. Australia penetration is projected as more rapid than others due to a higher cultural willingness to try new technology. Scandinavia and the Benelux are expected to be more receptive to the products initially, so their growth is faster. Japan will be slower because of the translation and conversion problems.

Nature of the Proposed Distribution Channel(s)

What kind of channels you will employ: exclusive or nonexclusive, owned or third-party?

Channel Conflict

How will you deal with potential conflicts?

Revenue Projection

The following example is based on the above projected territory rollout schedule:

Sample International Sales Revenue Projection
(in thousands)

Fiscal Year	1997	1998	1999	Total
Gross Revenue	$905	$3,421	$6,575	$10,900
Net Revenue	283	1,566	3,045	4,894
Costs	269	691	1,128	2,089
Direct Contribution	14	874	1,917	2,806

Annual Sales Projection by Territory over 3 Years

Cost of Sales and Direct Margin

Cost of Localization

Legal Costs

Investment Required

Revenue Plan

Staffing Plan

Support Plan Income and Expense Projection

Financial Models Including ROI (Return on Investment)

Staffing Plan

Risk Factors

Risks to the company in executing this plan include:

- Unstable foreign economies
- Fraud
- Division of management attention

Overall, these risks and considerations, while real, are quite manageable. They require consistent and careful management attention. When considered together with the corresponding major revenue potentials, the balance could provide a strong case for aggressive pursuit of the worldwide market.

Conclusion

The international business plan is a powerful tool to keep focus clear, to communicate expectations and goals internally, and to measure progress against expectations. Keep it current. The effort is well worthwhile.

Figure 4.1. Sample Territory Rollout Plan

Territory	Expected Entry Date	Expected First Sale	Cumulative Worldwide Market Coverage
United Kingdom	6/97	1/98	9%
Scandinavia	6/97	1/98	14%
Benelux	6/97	1/98	18%
Japan	7/98	4/99	32%
Australia/New Zealand	7/98	1/99	37%
Germany/Austria/ Switzerland	6/98	1/99	56%
Italy	6/99	1/00	65%
France	7/99	2/00	79%
Brazil	1/00	6/00	82%
Spain	1/00	7/00	85%
Other Latin America	7/00	2/01	87%

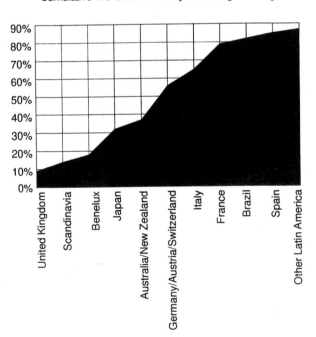

Cumulative Worldwide Territory Marketing Coverage

WORK THE PLAN

Now that you have a plan, follow it. It is daft to invest time and energy creating an appropriate plan for expanding your export business, then toss it out the window when the first unexpected opportunity knocks or when unanticipated difficulties are encountered. That is not to say that the plan must be a rigid mold for all future activities. As John Rome, Managing Director of Virginia-based Information Conveyances, Inc., often said, "I reserve the right to wake up smarter tomorrow."

So treat your business expansion trajectory as guided, not ballistic. Of course, midcourse corrections are allowed, in fact, necessary. Even if your planning was perfect given the facts at the time, the software business changes constantly, and at an ever-accelerating rate.

Just as you require your international channel partners to prepare a new territory marketing plan each year, so should you revise and update your own international business plan. And follow it.

Most Important Decisions Made Up Front

"The distributor selection process is time-consuming and difficult, but the costs of a bad decision in selecting distributors can far outweigh the expense and time it takes to select one properly in the first place," says William Fath in *How to Develop and Manage Successful Distributor Channels in World Markets* (p. 8).

Even though the urge to get on with it is strong, given the pressures of realizing the benefits of market expansion, the knowledge that competitors are out grabbing market share and that software products have limited lives, you must proceed at a deliberate and prudent pace. Make sure your homework is done before you jump into a long-term commitment. The time scales are simply longer when dealing internationally. As in baking a cake, you cannot rush it by turning up the heat.

Chapter 5

Electronic Export and Marketing
on the Internet

ELECTRONIC MARKETING

On-line commerce on the Internet is instantly global. Once up with an offer on your web site, you are technically doing business in over 150 countries.

The attraction of selling software electronically is that you have a product that can be advertised, marketed, ordered, paid for, and delivered, all on-line, and at a nearly negligible cost per transaction. Entry into foreign markets is, in theory at least, greatly simplified.

No longer is market entry into one country at a time. But there are some caveats. For one, if in the United States you are encrypting, say, credit card information, you may be in violation of the government's International Traffic in Arms Regulations (see Chapter 3). For another, you may encounter decency laws which are more stringent than those of the United States. Countries including China, Germany, and Singapore have sanctioned on-line service providers for content that is legal in the United States. Transmission of personal information is also subject to special protection in some countries, especially within the European Union.

THE WEB SITE

Probably the most attractive medium to begin your electronic distribution is the Internet's World Wide Web.

Construction

Domain Name

Register your chosen domain name with InterNic as soon as possible, even if you are not yet ready to begin site construction. The good names are being grabbed up quickly.

Language Issues

Remember, your site will be read all over the world. A truly international site will give the reader a choice on the home page of what language the session will be displayed. Remember to display each language choice itself in that language. For some languages, this will lead you into the world of double-byte characters (see Chapter 1).

Security

If you are a U.S. company, you currently cannot equip your customers or distribution channel outside the country with decryption software using greater than forty-bit keys. Forty-bit key encryption can be broken quite easily. So if you intend to put licensed material on your web site, you will need to rely on other security methods.

Among other methods that are usable:

- *Password protection.* This can be effective if:
  - The passwords are changed frequently.
  - Passwords are at least six characters long including upper- and lower-case letters and numbers.
  - The birthdays of all relatives are avoided.
- *Token-based protection.* A token can be a small handheld random-number generator synchronized with the firewall server. Looking like a pocket calculator, it generates a new random key every, say, sixty seconds. That random key, along with the user's ID and the user's own password, are needed to access the site. This method is quite secure, as long as lost or stolen tokens are reported promptly. SecureID of Boston, MA, sells such devices.

Promoting the Site

The site will have to be promoted, not only on all your marketing literature, stationery, and business cards, but in your ads and mailings as well. Contests, free stuff, valuable information, and entertainment can all be used to attract visitors. Wording the home page in such a way that it will index well in search engines such as Yahoo, AltaVista, HotBot, and the like is important. Include all the keywords that someone might use to try to find your site.

Without additional promotion, though, it is doubtful that search engines alone will result in enough hits to make your site profitable.

Obtaining Hot Links

Your site should link to those of your channel partners, and vice versa. Hardware and software vendors of those platforms and products you support should also point to yours. This may involve becoming a member of one of their partner programs.

Similarly, you may be able to negotiate mutual web page linkages with vendors of products complementary to your own.

Ad Sharing

Dr. Marc Slack of Mitre Corp. suggests the following (personal communication, 1996): negotiate with owners of other sites that might attract qualified buyers of your product. When those owners put links into their sites pointing to yours, you can capture the resulting visits to your site, and pay the site owners a small "referral" fee for each hit. If the visit results in a customer, a higher "commission" will be paid. This not only provides incentive for the complementary site to include your link, but to make it attractive and inviting to explore. Of course, such arrangements can be bidirectional.

ELECTRONIC DISTRIBUTION

Shareware

Few companies have yet made a profit selling directly over the Internet. However, the classic success story of Netscape, which got its start by making its software freely available on the net and then went on to an initial public offering valuing the company at close to U.S. $1 billion, must give rise to serious thought.

Many firms offer downloadable software on the Web. Most of that is free, but comes with a plea from the vendor that the user, if satisfied, send in a small license fee, typically U.S. $5 to $50. Few ever do. This is the shareware approach. But as Netscape and a few others have proved, if you can get the market hooked on the entry-level free product, it is possible to build a real business selling a feature-rich follow-on version of the same product.

On-Line Distribution

Regardless of how you license your product, you may wish to distribute it over the Internet by permitting downloads by authorized users. This requires that your product not be too large. Products larger than about five megabytes are today inconvenient for the casual, modem-connected user to download.

You can also distribute product updates via the Web. Intuit, for example, has an excellent site that permits legitimate customers to download updated modules to Quicken; these modules fix lists of known problems and add specific capabilities. This is done without further cost to Intuit or the customer, and surely saves the company millions in telephone support and mailing costs.

Getting Paid

If you do choose to actually sell product licenses over the Internet, you want to be sure to get paid. There is today an uneasiness on the part of many would-be customers about transmitting credit card numbers over the Internet. Yes, they can be snooped and misused. But the same thing can happen in many nonelectronic ways.

There are also a number of approaches to secure such transactions. Netscape comes with a secure communication mode. Cybercash is coming to market with an "electronic wallet" of secure cash that customers can spend over the net from their previously established bank accounts. Jriver Corp. in Minneapolis, MN, licenses a product called Rover which uses a Windows 95 Explorer-like interface to allow the user to locate, pay for, and download software products. Their web site is *http//:www.jriver.com*.

Dealing with known customers, you can simply invoice via e-mail and ask for a check, or permission to debit their previously disclosed credit card number.

On-Line Support

Offering support on-line is a very attractive way to fulfill, at least partially, your requirement to help both your distribution channel and your customers worldwide. You may choose which parts of your web site are open to the public, which to customers and which only to the channel. Access to these sections can be controlled with passwords.

Beyond putting a list of known bugs and other problems into a readily accessible form, and beyond providing downloadable fixes, or even updated product versions, you can aid your channel by allowing access to your internal help desk system.

Your channel is on the firing line in the market, representing you to prospects and customers. The more accurate, up-to-date information they can obtain about progress in fixing problems reported to you, the better job they can do. If they can spot that the same problem has already been reported but not yet fixed, you will save the cost of their establishing a new problem report.

Whether you use a commercial help desk product such as Vantive or Remedy or a home-grown system, let your channel partners have read-only access to the data base, preferably via the Internet. Better, let them input problem descriptions and priorities in their own time zones and locations, so that when your level-two support staff reports to work, the traditional morning paperwork is already done, and they can get right to work solving customer problems.

Beyond dealing with technical problems, the net can be an excellent and cost-effective way for your foreign channel partners to submit orders to you for products, literature, manuals, brochures, and anything else they want to pay for. Many such requests can be electronically fulfilled, saving shipping cost and time, and facilitating language translation if required on the receiving end. E-mail can be used for most kinds of written communications, including forecasts, sales reports, requests for passwords, and reporting product bugs. It is time to eliminate faxes from the world!

Chapter 6

Managing the Channel

MARKET COMMITMENT

To a large degree, your success in each foreign market will be proportional to the long-term commitment your company makes to that market. Developing markets takes time and capital. Only "bleeding edge" technologists are comfortable buying software never tried and unknown in the territory. Getting those first few or few hundred sales can be difficult and expensive.

Neither the channel nor the customer will make these necessary investments if there is any perception that you will not be around for the long haul. Be conscious of your communications and your actions, and what message they convey. Most foreign markets have very little tolerance of the "slash and burn" marketing tactics popular with some U.S. firms who run through a market, pick some low hanging fruit, and then move on or disappear.

One important way you will both demonstrate and accomplish committing to a market is by setting up a permanent, rational structure to manage your worldwide channel.

ORGANIZATIONAL RESPONSIBILITIES

Firms committed to export have not only an individual responsible for those activities, but a department. Responsibilities such as channel development, sales and technical training, order fulfillment, territory marketing, and financial management all have a place in the international department.

Companies have used a variety of organizational structures. Certainly you send an important signal to your foreign market when you appoint a senior executive to manage export sales. Two common flavors are vice president international, and president or managing director of a wholly-owned subsidiary devoted to export. Company "X," for instance, may incorporate "X International" to be its export arm. The president of X International is then responsible for the export business.

To whom should the international business report? Common options are: to the CEO; to the VP of sales and marketing, if there is one; and to the VP of sales. Any of these options can work, but if the export manager's boss has no international experience, the export operation will be handicapped.

When export business exceeds a certain volume, it probably makes sense to regionalize it. Some firms such as CA International and Sterling Software have separate management structures for direct and indirect channels. Others divide the world into two, three, or half a dozen geographical regions, each with its regional manager. Needless to say, the regional manager for Latin America should speak Spanish and, preferably, Portuguese. The East Asia manager would speak Japanese at a minimum. And so forth.

Herman J. Maggiori discusses organizing for export in his comprehensive book, *How to Make the World Your Market*. While not always appropriate for the software firm, he advances some worthy suggestions.

Whatever way you organize it, make sure there are enough of your own people watching out for and managing the international business.

EVENTS AND INCENTIVES

Geoffrey A. Moore wrote in *Crossing the Chasm*, "Getting and sustaining the attention of someone else's sales force is a full-time job, since helping to sell someone else's product is an unnatural act which must be restimulated continually" (p. 134). Though the context was slightly different, this truth applies equally to international software distribution.

Partner Conferences

Probably the most important event for your channel is the partner conference. Whether the attendees are third-party distributors, VARs, subsidiary employees, or a combination, such conferences, properly planned and executed, are invaluable for imparting sales tips, absorbing market intelligence, and stimulating excitement and productivity in the channel.

A partner conference should be held at a minimum annually. Some prefer to hold them at the vendor's headquarters, others at varying locations around the world. In favor of the former are lower travel cost for the vendor and easy access to all key vendor personnel and facilities. On the other hand, the exotic location can stimulate attendance (many distributors like to combine business with pleasure), and enhance the impact of the experience. Remember, with third-party channel partners, keeping share of mind is the major battle.

Other choices are whether to invite only senior partner managers; sales and technical managers; all sales staff; or everyone. Inviting spouses is also common. The general rule is that attendees cover their own travel costs, but there are exceptions. The vendor host will generally plan an information-filled agenda, with plenty of opportunity for interaction, plus gala dinners, receptions, bands, welcome gifts, engraved conference binders, side trips to enjoyable locations, boat cruises, and local fun diversions. These events may consume a large portion of the annual international marketing budget, and be well worth it.

The location should be relatively easy to get to. An obscure European town that requires two air legs from major European capitals, plus a long taxi ride will generally draw complaints. Some popular venues are Paris, the Canary Islands, Vienna, Istanbul, Copenhagen, Capetown, Bermuda, Sydney, and any of the Mediterranean Riviera towns. Many Asians and Latin Americans welcome an opportunity to visit Europe on business—not necessarily a reciprocal feeling.

Good, professional organization is essential. If you lack this experience on your staff, or do not have the time for organizing such an event (minimum of 300 hours), professional event organizers can do the job for you. Plan on sending out invitations at least six months in advance, with a detailed agenda to follow within eight weeks. Most business people will not travel abroad without a detailed agenda to reassure them that the trip will be worthwhile.

Do not start daily agendas before 0900: most of the world is not used to working earlier hours. And do not plan a succession of long days of lecture presentations. Not only is it boring, but many nonnative speakers will reach mental burnout after listening to more than a few hours of any foreign language presentation.

Be sure there are plenty of company representatives present during the entire event, at least one host for every two guests. Company folks should be instructed to spend break and meal times mingling with the foreign guests, not socializing with each other.

One or more pre-event meetings with all the company participants to coordinate roles and go over ground rules are essential. This will be a major investment of time and money for all concerned, and must be carried off with almost military precision to be considered fully successful. Control the schedule. Your agenda is a time contract with the attendees. Do not let speakers run over, and keep to the posted times. The attendees will respect and appreciate this.

Sales Kickoffs

Every year, or more often if new products are flowing quickly out of development or through acquisition, a sales kickoff should be held. These may be global, regional, or by territory, depending on the size of the sales force.

The purpose should be to teach about the new products, how to sell and support them, and to build enthusiasm for them. The kickoff may be an integral part of the new product launch. Attendance should include the entire channel sales and sales support staffs.

Kickoffs also benefit from the frills mentioned in the previous section, but may also be done plainly and unadorned if they are thorough, professional, and most of all, enthusiastic.

Quota Clubs

The reward of all-expense paid travel to a resort location with one's spouse included to participate in group and individual recognition and fun can be the strongest motivator available to salespeople. Many firms use quota clubs (a.k.a., President's Clubs, Golden Circles, 100 Percent Clubs, Achievers Clubs, etc.) as domestic sales incentives. A comparable benefit can be obtained by offering such incentives to the international channel as well.

There are several considerations when offering participation to third-party channel partners:

- Try to make sure that the actual salespeople responsible for outstanding sales of your products are the ones invited, not their bosses or the owners of the company (unless they are doing the selling).
- Think carefully about setting targets for the partner company as a whole versus individual salesperson targets. The latter may be difficult to police outside your own organization.
- Set the sales hurdle high enough so that there is enough margin to justify the expense of the club, allowing for the fact that you as the sponsor are receiving only the net or discounted revenue figure.
- Make sure that targets are not set such that the whole promotion becomes a disincentive for salespeople in smaller territories who cannot possibly achieve the numbers.
- There are advantages to inviting both domestic and foreign winners to the same club. The event gains more critical mass, and the participants can informally share successes and sales secrets along the way.

The club can be for a long weekend or a full week. Do not schedule it during peak selling time (typically fourth calendar quarter), or too long after the end of the quota year, lest the cause-and-effect incentive be lost.

Sales and Technical Training Courses

You should offer sales training to your channel:

- Whenever you introduce a new product
- Whenever you figure out a better way to sell your products
- Whenever you reposition your product or your company
- When a channel partner does not seem to be keeping up with the rest of the world in sales productivity
- At least once a year

Courses can be at the home office, regionally, or at the distributor's location. It is best to hold them out of the office to minimize distractions. Use your top trainers, as this training will be leveraged in the field. Field technicians should receive all sales training courses as well as technical ones, because anyone in contact with customers or prospects is selling.

These courses can be fun. They can be held at exotic locations, with some time given for recreation. You will have to find a balance that will attract the maximum number of channel participants. If it looks too frivolous, channel partners will be reluctant to spend the money to have their people taking sales time out of the territory.

Spiffs

Giving cash or merchandise awards directly to channel salespeople who successfully sell your product is, if not subtle or creative, a time-honored and effective way to grab their attention. Make sure the margins justify the costs. Expect objections from partner management who may see such programs as usurping management control of their own sales staff.

Sales Contests

You can be very creative here, and such contests, if properly promoted, can be effective motivators. Categories can be such as first sale of a new product, largest sale, or most sales volume per salesperson. Be careful to equalize the contest. Greece competing with Germany for total sales volume will usually not be motivational due to the vast difference in territory potential.

Gifts and Prizes

When you visit them, when they visit you, at sales meetings, when they sign as a new distributor, when an especially important sale is closed—these are all appropriate times to give a gift. Usually something tasteful, useful, and coming from your home country is most appreciated. There is no need to get lavish, though lavish might be called for. One company offered a new Lexus or BMW to the first salesperson worldwide to break U.S. $1 million in sales each year. This was considered worthwhile, and was a great motivator.

Visit Jack Nadel's section on "Making Your Distributor Work Hard" on page 178 in *Cracking the Global Market* for additional ideas on channel motivation.

SUPPORTING THE CHANNEL

Support Requirements

In the startup phase particularly, support requirements will be critical to the speed of market development, and could impact domestic sales. New distributors will need to be trained, and are least capable of supporting their customers unassisted. As they mature, their support requirements lessen considerably, and become more predictable.

You may choose to have international technical product specialists who will assist distribution partners with training, seminar presentations, sales calls, and installation problems. International administrative assistants can handle details of contract administration, travel and event planning, personnel allocation, and correspondence. They will provide continuity of contact for a frequently-traveling staff, thus allowing for a better level of partner service. International marketing specialists work with channel partners to plan, coordinate, and optimize each marketing program in the territory.

Because technical and marketing needs of international may be sporadic, you may find it uneconomical to staff for the peaks. Some use, therefore, might be made of domestic systems engineers and marketing specialists during territory startup.

European, Asian, and Latin American regional support centers should be considered when the respective region reaches a minimum level in gross sales.

The European regional office might be located in the United Kingdom or the Netherlands. The United Kingdom has lower costs and a more liberal (from the employer's point of view) labor laws. The Netherlands, on the other hand, is more centrally located than the United Kingdom, is in same time zone as the rest of western Europe, and staff are more likely to speak German, French, English, and of course, Dutch. The Dutch tax treaties are among the most favorable in Europe. Other attractive European candidate countries are France for its central location, Denmark for its incentives, and Ireland for its low labor costs.

Design your collateral to be used worldwide. See Appendix 6, "Checklist When Writing for an International Audience."

Postpaid return-mail postcards will not work from abroad, except within the EU.

MANAGING MULTIPLE CHANNEL ENTITIES/APPROACHES IN A TERRITORY

In order to optimize your distribution, you may choose to mix approaches within a single market. You may have both a direct and an indirect channel; multiple nonexclusive distributors; an exclusive partner for one product line and nonexclusive VARs for another; and so on. This can be fine, but it invites management problems. If anticipated, with "rules of engagement" clearly spelled out for all players in advance, these approaches can work.

Avoiding Channel Conflict

Of course, you want your distribution channel to compete with the competition, not with itself. Yet if several parties can all sell your product to the same customer, the result can be price cutting, lower profits, and lower investment in the market. No one distributor will run an ad that will benefit others selling the same product in the territory. No third party wants to compete directly with its supplier, as there is a natural disadvantage in margin, if nothing else.

There are many classical ways to solve this problem, none peculiar to international arena:

- Private label the products, so that the customer does not readily perceive the competition. This may be as involved as repackaging the product and its documentation, and changing splash screens, HELP text, and imbedded literals which identify the product by name.
- Employ a lead registration system. Each partner can have exclusive rights to sell to a specific customer for ninety days after the prospect is first registered with you.

- Divide the market by deal size. Microsoft agrees not to compete directly with it VARs for deals under $10 million.
- "Double Bubble." Your direct sales force receives the same commission whether the product is sold directly or through a VAR in their territory. This reduces margin, of course, but can create phenomenal cooperation between the VARs and your salespeople.
- Bundling. Some of your channel partners agree to resell your products only as a larger package of items, or with a particular value added, thus eliminating direct competition.

Dividing Up the Product Line

Some product lines may be more appropriate for exclusive or direct representation. A relatively compact, easily identified market can be worked efficiently by a single entity. Other lines may be targeted at a widely dispersed, poorly organized market, such as small businesses or individuals. Multiple local channel partners will likely be needed in this case. If your firm has lines in both categories, you may wish to consider employing both approaches.

Master VAR/Distributor

A kind of hybrid approach would be the appointment of a master VAR or distributor who would then appoint and manage other VARs or subdistributors to help cover the market. It is then up to the master to minimize intrachannel competition within the territory. Depending on the size of the market, such an arrangement could be either exclusive or nonexclusive.

ASSURING COMPLIANCE WITH EXPORT CONTROLS

Even though you once might have diligently established your export business in full compliance with the law, it is a good idea to periodically audit operations to make sure that the passage of time and changing procedures have not put you out of compliance. Conduct an internal audit every so often to ensure that your export licensing procedures are correct: changes in the law and in your product line might have invalidated your old approach.

Also critical is assurance that you are not in inadvertent violation of the U.S. Foreign Corrupt Practices Act. Make sure that your procedures prohibit not only your employees (some of whom may be newly hired foreign nationals in your new subsidiaries and unfamiliar with this unique U.S. law) from bribing officials, but that your indirect sales channel is also so restricted.

Bring in legal counsel for a day to help conduct this review. The payoff can be major. You may even find that you can now simplify procedures because of recent relaxations of export restrictions.

MONITORING PROGRESS

Track Results

As in any business, tracking and measuring progress is key to management. Just because your channel is far away and speaks a different language does not excuse them from the kind of reporting you need to manage them. With timely information in hand, you can accurately forecast sales, take prompt corrective action when needed, and continuously evaluate progress.

There are at least four major report types needed, as follows. Your business may require more.

Annual Sales Plan

This is a two-year plan, indicating how the channel partner intends to market and sell your products over the period. It should include territory plans for advertising, trade shows, direct mail, seminars, and other activities. Changes in the makeup of the sales force and the support structure should be outlined. Budgets for each activity should be spelled out, and forecasted quarterly sales revenue indicated.

The sales plan gives you an opportunity to understand a partner's intentions, and to work with her in a meaningful way to "tune up" and optimize the plan in light of your knowledge of what is and is not working worldwide, and of your company's product and promotional plans during the period.

The Annual Sales Plan is applicable equally to company-owned and independent channel partners.

Annual Financial Report

It is especially important to insist on an annual financial report from each partner. From this you can judge if there are impending financial problems that might jeopardize future receivables, whether or not the partner will likely have the cash available to finance the Sales Plan, and, indeed, whether the partnership is actually profitable for the partner. If it is not, something will have to change. It is better if that change is initiated by, rather than inflicted on, you.

Many countries require every corporation to file an annual financial statement which becomes a matter of public record. Your international accounting firm can help you to obtain copies of these filings. Since you will not always receive audited financial statements from your independent channel partners, these public reports serve as a good cross-check on the financial information you receive.

Monthly Financial Reports

From your owned channel operations and joint ventures you should certainly obtain monthly income statements, balance sheets, and cash flow reports. These give an inside look at many factors you will need to properly manage those businesses. Do not normally expect foreign independent partners to be willing to furnish financial data this frequently, however.

Sales Forecasts

The ninety-day sales forecast is the heart of the reporting system. From this you can see how the pipeline is building, close ratios, and what the level of business is likely to be. After a period of time you can calibrate the accuracy of these reports, and begin to be able to precisely manage your export business.

You can also see where the problems are, and obtain a view on how to more effectively support the partner. If not enough prospects come into the pipeline, perhaps a cooperative advertising campaign or joint seminars are in order. If few trials are closing, perhaps more product sales or technical training is needed.

After a year of doing business, it is not difficult to build a simple statistical model for each partner correlating forecasted and actual sales. A linear regression model always looking back over each of the past twelve months of forecasted and actual sales will give you a correlation factor. The closer that factor is to one, the more linear the forecast is. That is, the forecast may be consistently too high or too low, but it can be corrected by multiplying by a constant and adding another constant.

Apply linear regression to the aggregate of all your channels' forecasts, and you will begin to be able to predict quite accurately what the following month's business will be.

The channel should be able to supply a new ninety-day forecast at the beginning of each month. Figure 6.1 is a model of what this report might look like.

Sales Reports

Also at the beginning of each month, actual sales for the previous month should be reported. Here will be the end results of all the steps outlined in this book. The total of sales reported on these forms can be fed into you accounting system as the month's gross international sales. If you invoice from partner sales, this report drives the invoicing process. It should show the customer name, value of the sale, and the name and quantity of products licensed. A model sales report is shown in Figure 6.2.

Billing and Collection

A key part of your export operation will be management of accounts receivable. Be sure you get your invoices out on time and are aggressive in chasing any overdue payments. Watching the pattern of receivables and tracking days of sales outstanding can tell you a lot about the financial health and relative enthusiasm of your channel partners.

Figure 6.1. Sample Ninety-Day Sales Forecast

Report prepared by:_____   Date:_____

Prospect Name	Prospect City	License Type	Product Codes	Price in Local Currency	Net Royalty $ U.S.	Est. Close Month	Status Code

License Types		Product Codes	Status Codes	
P	Permanent		P	Prospect
R	Rental		I	Installed Trial
LP	Lease/Purchase		C	Contract Negotiation
U	Upgrade			

PERSPECTIVE

Long Time Frames—Think in Terms of Years

Establishing an international distribution network is not an overnight process. Recall the joke about the guy parachuting into the Brazilian jungle with the mission from his boss to set up a chain of supermarkets within the month. Some things just take time, especially with limited resources.

Figure 6.2. Sample Monthly Sales Report

Report prepared by:_____   Date:_____

Customer Name	Customer City	Customer Number	Product Codes	Price in Local Currency	Net Royalty $ U.S.	Effective Date or Period	Trans-action Type Code

Product Codes	Transaction Type Codes	
	S	Single Payment License
	U	Upgrade
	R	Rental or Lease Payment
	M	Maintenance

The trading mentality in most countries is much more relationship-oriented than in the United States. Relationships cannot be built in a day, and neither can international trade. The temptation to hurry and to cut corners may be high if there is uninformed pressure from the top to achieve unrealistically short-term sales goals. The damage done by selecting the wrong distributor in a key territory will last for years, and may never be fully reparable.

Be methodical. Plan. Take time to do it right. Realistically, unless your product is "in the tornado" as Geoffrey Moore would say, years rather than months will be required to achieve a substantial contribution to your top line from software export. But once that channel is built, if it is well maintained, it will continue to serve you with high-margin revenues for many years to come.

Flameouts and Damage Control

Expect setbacks and be prepared for failures, even spectacular ones, among your distribution channels. Bankruptcy, fraud, death, dissolution, and flagrant neglect are all possibilities. The more closely you monitor the channel, the less surprised you will be. But you obviously cannot prevent all such occurrences.

Therefore, it is best to have backup plans in one's pocket. Part of your job of managing each territory is not only to work to optimize the performance of the existing channel, but always to be cultivating possibilities for alternative channels as well. Get to know all possible distributors and VARs in the territory, even those of competitors. Thus if you have to replace a channel partner, you will not have to start from scratch.

But note that replacing a major or exclusive partner could have significant unfavorable repercussions in the territory. The event may call into doubt in the eyes of the market your commitment, staying power, judgment, and reputation. These effects may be redoubled if you part on bad terms and the former partner makes its displeasure known publicly in the marketplace. Be assured that your competitors will attach the worst possible spin to the changeover. And a series of failed distribution relationships is that much worse. After a certain point (say, more than two major partners within five years), the market may no longer take you or your products with any seriousness at all.

For these reasons, changing major partners (as opposed to changing one or two of ten nonexclusive VARs in a territory, for example) should be avoided if at all possible. The opposite can hold true when establishing a direct presence where you were previously indirect. In this situation, much positive PR can be made of the fact that the territory is important enough to require a direct investment; that customers will receive better service dealing directly with you, the original vendor.

Meet and stay in contact with top salespeople, sales managers, and technical people in the territories. If you later decide to establish a direct presence there, you will have a group of known people from which to offer key positions.

COMMUNICATION

What you communicate with your channel partners serves to position the nature of the relationship. As *partners*, they will want to know whom they are doing business with: the good, the bad, and the ugly. After all, you most likely require financial information from them. If you are a public company, providing financial data is not an issue. But many private companies are close to the vest with their financial numbers. Share those numbers, at least in summary, with your distribution channel. They need to become comfortable with making investments in your future. If the numbers are not good, then your explanation of why and how they will improve is vital to the nature of the relationship.

Share also your goals, strategies, product plans, and direction. Under a nondisclosure agreement, of course, but do communicate with your partners, lest you ignore William Fath's admonition (in *How to Develop and Manage Successful Distributor Channels in World Markets,* p. 34): "If you consider the distributors merely as customers for your products, then forget about using the distributor sales channel. You won't be successful!"

MEASUREMENT AND FEEDBACK

You cannot manage what you do not measure. This wise old axiom is doubly true of a far flung, worldwide operation. You surely are not there to see, touch, and feel everywhere every day, as your domestic counterparts might be. So you need feedback.

Beyond the standard management financial reports of revenues, costs, accounts receivable, and profits, you need a feel for how the business is going. How is your company perceived in the market-place? How do your channel partners evaluate you against other suppliers they might represent?

One way of getting at this information is regularly taking surveys—ask your channel partners in a structured way, "How am I doing?" Have them rate you in a variety of categories: responsiveness, quality of product, effectiveness of communication, price competitiveness, and so forth. Tally the results and keep a running comparison. If you start tailing off in a category, find out why and correct the trend. Capitalize on your strengths. You could collect the same sort of information from your owned operations, although it might not be as objective.

Most important, though, is visiting. There is no substitute for being there. The International Director for a top-100 U.S. software company never traveled abroad, except to Europe, even though half the company's foreign sales came from other continents. Needless to say, this person's tenure in the job was not long.

In any case, you should not be managing international sales unless you have a zest for travel, a love for other cultures, and thrive on the excitement of the thousand variations in which business (and pleasure) is done around the world.

. . .

Too often I would hear men boast only of the miles covered that day, rarely of what they had seen.

—*Louis L'Amour*

Appendix 1

Characteristics
of the International Company

The international company:

- Perceives a world market for its products and services

    — understands that its largest market may be abroad
    — knows the relevant demographics of foreign territories

- Looks worldwide for sources of new technology, new products, new ideas, new techniques
- Is sensitive at all levels to the cultural differences of the nationalities

    — employs foreign nationals in management and on the board of directors
    — values employee foreign language skills—rewards them and pays for their acquisition

- Recognizes, plans for, and arranges business to accommodate trans-oceanic time zone distances

    — time-buffers corporate and customer communication

- Is prepared to do business in foreign currencies
- Uses legal and financial counsel with international competence

    — recognizes that local counsel is essential for foreign operations

- Complies with international standards (e.g., ISO; the metric system)
- Considers the international implications of all corporate communications and decisions

Appendix 2

Case Study

Introduction

In 1994, Senator John McCain presented the President's "E" Award to Viasoft Inc., a Phoenix, Arizona firm, for excellence in export. Viasoft was one of only four software companies to have won in the twenty-odd-year history of the award. Viasoft today is a public company with fiscal 1996 sales of over U.S. $43 million. Here is how Viasoft entered the export market and developed it into a major revenue contributor.

Founded in 1983, Viasoft developed and marketed software products for professional computer programmers and analysts. These products comprised an integrated set of tools to aid in understanding, maintaining, and redeveloping COBOL business applications.

The first product was introduced in 1986. The company added about one new product a year in the meantime. This integrated set of products was called the Existing Systems Workbench (ESW). It was used by organizations that operated large IBM and other mainframe computers to measure, analyze, edit, test, document, and reengineer their own business applications. Since 60 percent to 80 percent of most large companies' application programming work concerns existing systems, and this was an area that had been poorly supported by tools in the past, there was a reasonable and growing demand for Viasoft products.

The original ESW toolset itself ran exclusively on mainframe computers. Later, Viasoft developed PC-based front-ends for the ESW components which allowed professional users to access ESW via personal computers. All the company's products were developed by software engineers at the company's headquarters in Phoenix, although several products were based on technology purchased or licensed from abroad. Viasoft's products were accompanied by user manuals and instructional aids. The products were shipped to customers on magnetic tape cartridges.

Most of the company's revenue came from the sale of licenses. Typical ESW license fees ranged from U.S. $80,000 to $250,000 depending on the components selected and the size of the customer's computers. The second-largest revenue component was maintenance. Maintenance contracts, for which the customer paid an annual fee, provided telephone support, and all updates made by Viasoft to the products during the year.

Early History—The Ad Hoc Years

1986 and prior—All inquiries from abroad were carefully filed. Any chance international business was handled out of CEO's back pocket. A strictly reactive business.

1987—A technology licensing deal was done with a United Kingdom company. In return for rights to key technology, Viasoft gave cash, stock, and exclusive marketing rights for existing products in the United Kingdom, Benelux, and Scandinavia. This proved not to be a good way to open these markets for the company's products, as the technology company lacked adequate marketing and sales capabilities. No Viasoft sales were made in those territories that year.

1988—The company launched an unsuccessful search for a pan-European distributor. Only a few candidates were identified, and the preferred one already carried a competitor's product.

International as an Intentional Business

Despite the fact that about half of its potential market lay outside North America, Viasoft had sales within only the United States and Canada during its first five years of existence. In 1989, the company became proactive and began focusing on international opportunities. A full-time general manager was hired to develop the overseas markets for the company. The first step was the development of a comprehensive marketing plan, which in turn required a great deal of research.

Market Research

The research focused on three areas: demographics; distribution channels; and legal and financial considerations.

Demographics

Market size for Viasoft was determined primarily by the population of IBM and compatible mainframe computers, and secondarily by the operating system and programming languages used on those computers. Outside the

United States, this information was very difficult to find. The data was eventually assembled by gathering bits and pieces of information from many sources: published articles; and interviews with consultants, potential distributors, prospective customers, and other software companies. It showed the estimated number of sites in each territory which had the appropriate hardware and software environment to be able to use its products. The total export market was estimated at just over 5,000 sites. By comparison, in 1989 there were about an equal number of qualified sites in the United States. The worldwide market for system software (Viasoft's category) in 1987 was $19 billion, growing at an annual rate of 24 percent, the fastest growth rate of any computer-related segment. These statistics indicated an excellent potential market abroad, and helped to prioritize international efforts.

Audit and Accountability

Viasoft planned that its distributors would not be stocking distributors, but would be licensed to copy the software as needed. The following steps were identified to be taken with distributors to assure contract compliance: careful reference checking prior to entering into a business arrangement; frequent visits from Viasoft management to the distributor and its customers; attendance and intelligence gathering by Viasoft at international trade shows where customers would be likely to attend; periodic submission of certified financial reports; and formal periodic audits, both by the distributor's auditors and by a local firm retained by Viasoft.

Research Results

Other areas researched included revenue recognition and foreign withholding. The plan did not take into account the possibility of major changes in the worldwide business climate, political instabilities, or fluctuations in currency exchange rates. It also failed to consider the marketability of the company's products in foreign environments and languages. Luckily, this proved not to be a major problem, except in Japan.

Overall, however, these and the other risks and considerations, while real, were felt to be quite manageable. When considered together with the major revenue potential, they made a strong case for aggressive pursuit of the worldwide market. As a result of this research, Viasoft realized that much planning and many steps would be needed to ensure a smooth international operation. But none of the steps seemed insurmountable.

Development of a Distributor Network

From market research, the company was able to prioritize the territories it wanted to enter. The four major European markets of the United Kingdom, France, Germany, and Italy, plus Japan and Australia, were at the top of the list. Although it used a direct sales force in the United States and Canada, based on research, the company concluded that overseas, distributors would provide the fastest market entry at the least cost and risk.

The company chose exclusive arrangements initially because of the relatively small markets and high investment required in staffing and training in each country. Each distributor did its own marketing, sales, and first-level customer support. Distributors accessed headquarters by fax or telephone for second-level technical support. Since the products had been successful in the United State, and the company was offering exclusive, multiyear distributorships, Viasoft had considerable interest from potential distributors in most countries investigated.

Viasoft decided to appoint one distributor for each major country, or group of countries, representing at least 250 prospects sites. To be realistic, the plan was based on the necessity of replacing one established distributor each year.

In order to proceed quickly in establishing distribution in Germany and France, consultants were retained to assist in locating the most appropriate firms and to assist in developing a profile of the ideal distributor. After this initial experience, Viasoft was able to locate distributors in other countries without using outside consultants, sometimes with the help of the Department of Commerce. After thorough investigation, the company entered into negotiations with two or three distributors in each country simultaneously so as to promote competition for the product line and produce the most advantageous contract terms. Each of the finalists was requested to develop a marketing plan for the products.

In early 1990, it became clear that the original technology company in the United Kingdom was not going to be a player in Viasoft's international distribution plans. The unpleasant task of unwinding those distribution rights was accomplished that year. During 1990 and 1991, Viasoft appointed twelve distributors altogether covering most of western Europe, Japan, Australia, New Zealand, Singapore, Hong Kong, Malaysia, Brazil, and Southern Africa. Experience proved that making the first few sales in a country was especially time-consuming. Initially there was no credibility for the products, and most firms did not want to be the first to buy. The plan allowed an average of six months between the signing of a new distributor and the first sale, with the actual time varying in practice from three months to nearly a year.

By the end of 1991, Viasoft had achieved its first $1 million in sales in a country outside North America, and had over seventy overseas customers. In 1992, international sales had its first $1 million sales month.

Distributor Support and Channel Communication

Viasoft found that quite a bit of distributor training and handholding was necessary initially, and patience was a must. In the startup phase, support requirements were critical to the speed of market development, and, due to limited available resources, could adversely impact domestic sales. To help distributors answer technical questions, especially in time zones remote from headquarters, the company established electronic bulletin board and mail systems that allowed exchange of information on a twenty-four-hour, seven-day basis. It also supported dialing into a customer's computer anywhere in the world to diagnose particularly difficult problems. Over time, the distributors become able to resolve about 90 percent of all technical support issues without access to Phoenix. This reduced the support requirements and investment for the company, which, when the distributor program began, was doing less than U.S. $5 million in annual revenue.

A major part of the international marketing program was two-way communication with the sales channel. Since Viasoft introduced a new product every year, each of which required sales and technical training as well as a marketing rollout, the company developed a very close relationship with its distributors. The company referred to them not as distributors but as International Partners.

Viasoft held two meetings annually, specifically to promote communication, enthusiasm and partnership. The first was the Viasoft International Partner (VIP) Conference, usually held in Europe, and intended for the senior management of the partner organization and of Viasoft. The company invited distributor spouses; Viasoft management often brought their own, and mixed business discussions with mutually enjoyable activities. One year, for example, it hosted the VIP Conference in the Canary Islands, with recreational activities including camel rides, with lots of picture taking.

The second annual conference was the Viasoft International Sales and Technical (VIST) Conference, usually held in Phoenix, and intended for distributor sales and technical management. The company used these events to help train partners to sell and support new technology; to learn from the partners what their markets liked and did not like about the products; and to accept their input into the product planning cycle, marketing program, and the strategic direction of the company. Viasoft also held an annual Executive Advisory Board, which included both domestic and foreign customer executives, again to foster communication between the company and the field.

Frequent visits from Viasoft personnel helped keep significant mind-share of the distributors. Each distributor was treated as a blend between a customer and a branch sales office. A win-win relationship was the goal, with a long-term mentality, assuming consistent performance. Visibility into the distributor's outlook was obtained by review of the marketing plan from each distributor, which was updated annually.

IBM Alliance

In 1992, Viasoft entered into a worldwide marketing agreement with IBM known as the International Alliance for AD/Cycle. Under this agreement, IBM was to promote and/or sell licenses for the company's products in many countries around the world. IBM became a nonexclusive distributor for Viasoft in sixteen Asia/Pacific countries. The negotiation leading up to this agreement was intense and time-consuming, and required reaching separate agreements with IBM national organizations on four continents. Unfortunately, AD/Cycle itself was an eventual market flop. It took an additional year to unwind this agreement, which, despite the allure at the time of the IBM name, proved only a time-sink and a distraction for Viasoft.

Opening of Overseas Offices

Viasoft established its first overseas operating subsidiary by acquiring the Waterfield Company, its distributor for Australia and New Zealand, at the end of 1990. It kept the Waterfield staff in place, and renamed the company Viasoft Pty. Ltd. Despite a very poor economy in Australia and New Zealand at that time, the company was profitable two of the next three years, with sales well over U.S. $1 million in the third year. Viasoft Pty. Ltd. had offices in Sydney and Melbourne, and was a full sales and support operation. ·

The company's first overseas sales support office was opened near Brussels at the end of 1991. This office supported European distributors with technical and marketing expertise. The company opened its second support office in Tokyo in 1992. Unlike the company's other foreign offices, this office was staffed with U.S. residents on temporary assignment, although they all spoke Japanese. This operation supported distributors in Japan, Korea, Taiwan, Thailand, and China.

The second subsidiary was established in January 1993 in the United Kingdom, when the distributor there went into receivership. The company quickly hired most of the distributor's Viasoft sales and support team, acquired the customer licenses, and began doing business in new offices near London and near Manchester as Viasoft International.

Most overseas employees were already product-trained when hired, as they had previously worked for the distributor of the products. To keep up their currency they frequently visited headquarters to attend technical classes and sales meetings. The company also held sales and technical courses in Europe several times a year for distributors and its foreign employees.

Participation in Overseas Trade Missions and at Trade Fairs

Viasoft participated in selected international trade shows in support of its distributors. Participation in such shows as CeBIT in Hannover, Germany, lent credibility to the company's products and provided visibility into competitive and market trends. It used U.S. Department of Commerce U.S. Foreign and Commercial Service assistance in gathering market information and the Agent/Distributor Service for locating distributors in Singapore and Brazil.

Competition

There was not much foreign competition to Viasoft products. An English company called Advanced Programming Techniques marketed a competing product throughout Europe and in the United States, but without a great deal of success. The greatest competition was from customer inertia, in getting large organizations to automate tasks using the products that they had been doing manually for years.

Territory Marketing

Viasoft assisted its distributors in determining how best to position the products in light of the current local perceptions and prejudices of the marketplace. The company also advised on communicating that positioning to the local trade press, to industry opinion leaders, and to the marketplace in general. The marketing program typically included seminars, publicity, direct mail, and advertising, where appropriate. Together with the distributors, the company organized an annual European press tour to announce new products and introduce Viasoft executives. With certain distributors they did cooperative advertising.

Localization

Localization, including translation of marketing collateral, was done by distributors and subsidiaries. As a result, there were many local versions of ads, mailers, brochures, and promotional kits. Usually, these were based on the version created by the headquarters marketing group, although some were entirely original. Viasoft products themselves were used by professional programmers who were mostly accustomed to reading English.

However, this was not true in Japan, an important market. Therefore, the products, including user manuals and training materials, were translated into Japanese by the distributor for use in that market. Also, in order to enable product use in countries that use Chinese characters (Kanji) or similar writing, such as Japan, Korea, China, and Taiwan, the company made a major product investment to allow processing of double-byte characters. After 1989, all the company's mainframe products were designed for double-byte characters and for easy translation by having all translatable items (primarily messages, HELP text, and user screens) in external tables.

Because of the high incidence of software piracy in certain southern European and Asian counties, the company put additional security features into its products. For example, the products were licensed to operate only on certain CPUs, and checked serial numbers programmatically to assure that they were indeed running on a licensed machine. Viasoft distributed products in encrypted form only, with passwords required for decryption. Expiration dates were also enforceable within the software for trial users, rentals, and leases.

Success

By 1993, net export revenues had grown to nearly $6 million, about 30 percent of the company's $19.5 million total revenue. On a gross revenue basis, the company did almost 50 percent of its new product sales that year outside the United States. The company had by then nearly 700 large corporate and government customers in twenty-four countries on five continents.

Senior management had given solid support to the international program for five years, and the company's investment paid off. A definite plan was laid out, and largely followed. Mistakes were made, but none was very costly.

The U.S. Department of Commerce recognized this three-year export success story with the President's "E" Award in 1994.

Appendix 3

Sample Distribution Agreement

This form of distribution agreement is provided to help you construct one suitable for your particular business, and for the particular territory involved. It may serve as a kind of checklist to help you determine if you have covered all the points you wish to cover in such an agreement, and at least one way of dealing with such points.

It is most certainly not the correct form of agreement as it stands for your specific situation. *No such agreement should be finalized without review of both local territory counsel and your own counsel.* There can be no standard agreement for all territories. Every country's laws are different, and these laws inevitably affect distribution agreements. Local counsel can make the appropriate recommendations.

This agreement is appropriate for high-priced, business-use software. The distributor is also a licensee, and is given an extensive set of rights and duties. For low-priced consumer software products, this form of agreement would probably not be suitable. In that case, an end-user shrink-wrap license would often suffice, and the distributor need not be named as a licensee.

Some pertinent points in this agreement are:

- It is an exclusive contract. This may or may not be best for your situation—distributors and VARs always ask for exclusives, but it may not be in your best interest to grant them. This form of agreement would be illegal in the European Union, where such exclusivity is considered anticompetitive. There are, however, other contractual ways of limiting territorial marketing activities in Europe that may achieve similar results. This is an essential area of concern for your local counsel.
- It provides for a buyout at a price either fixed or determined by the previous year's sales. The exit strategy is perhaps the most important part of a foreign software distribution contract.

- It provides for a quota to be met in order to be renewed annually. Be cautious about including recurring revenues such as maintenance in quotas. One distributor eventually obtained a virtually perpetual contract as the quota was less than the maintenance coming out of the territory. He had no further incentive to sell the company's products, and merely reaped an annuity by servicing the customer base with level-one support.
- This agreement specifies U.S. law. For a U.S. company, this will be a very helpful clause should a serious dispute arise, and is generally acceptable to the foreign distributor.
- The agreement does not call for arbitration. However, arbitration can be very effective, as well as much cheaper and quicker than lawsuits. It should be strongly considered. Binding arbitration is recognized by treaty and can be enforced in a large number of countries.

Term Summary

A summary of the significant terms, together with paragraph references to the contract, follows.

Parties

An agreement between independent contractors, VENDOR and the LICENSEE (2b), for the LICENSEE to market on an exclusive basis, certain VENDOR software programs in the Territory (2a). No sublicensees may be appointed (2a).

Exclusivity

No one (including VENDOR) except LICENSEE is permitted to market within the Territory, but hardware OEMs may, with a payment to the LICENSEE of 10 percent of VENDOR's net (2c).

Costs

All costs are to be borne by the LICENSEE including training, sales help, documentation, advertising, collateral, shipping, and translation (5a, 5b, 7c, 8b). Translated works to be owned by VENDOR (7c).

Quotas

Year 1 and 2 quotas are specified in Exhibit D. Subsequent years' quotas 150 percent of previous year.

Dedicated Personnel

The number of sales and technical are specified (7a).

Competitive Products

None is permitted to be handled by the LICENSEE (8d).

Reporting

The LICENSEE will prepare monthly sales reports and forecasts and an annual marketing plan (8j).

Up-Front Payment

A fee paid up-front by the LICENSEE will be credited against future payments (4c).

Termination by Either Party

For default, bankruptcy, or insolvency (13c).

Termination by VENDOR

For quota shortfall within the six months following each quota year (13b).
If LICENSEE's management or control changes contrary to the best interests of VENDOR (13d).
Without cause at any time by payment of a fixed sum or portion of last year's revenues (13e).

Termination (General)

All end-user contracts are assumable by VENDOR upon any termination (13g).

Revenue Split

LICENSEE pays VENDOR 50 percent of the greater of VENDOR's domestic list price or LICENSEE's actual price of sublicense and maintenance (4a). This amount is reduced to 40 percent for sales over quota (4f).

All payments to VENDOR by bank wire transfer at the conversion rate quoted by *The Wall Street Journal* at time of end-user contract execution (4d).

Joint Venture

The LICENSEE agrees, at VENDOR's option, to enter into good-faith negotiations on establishing a joint venture marketing VENDOR in the Territory (2e).

Boilerplate

Protections against government restrictions (5e); indemnification of liabilities (8q, 10); protection of intellectual property rights (11); choice of law (17).

Other Terms

Terms not covered in this agreement, but which may be required in particular cases include:

> ***Foreign Corrupt Practices Act.*** LICENSEE hereby certifies that neither it, its affiliates, nor any of its directors, officers, employees or agents is an official, agent, or employee of any government, governmental agency, or political party, or a candidate for any political office, on the date of this Agreement. LICENSEE shall promptly notify VENDOR of the occurrence of any event that would or may result in an exception to the foregoing representation. LICENSEE shall not, directly of indirectly, in the name of, or on behalf of, or for the benefit of itself or VENDOR, offer, promise, or authorize to pay, or pay any compensation, or give anything of value to, any official, agent, or employee of any government or governmental agency, or to any political party or officer, employee, or agent thereof, or to any candidate for political office. LICENSEE acknowledges that it has received and is familiar with VENDOR's company policy regarding the Foreign Cor-

rupt Practices Act (FCPA), is familiar with the FCPA, and warrants and represents to comply fully with the provision of such company policy and the FCPA as amended from time to time. VENDOR shall have the right to have access to information regarding the payments of any commissions or other funds by LICENSEE to any government official or agent. Any breach of the provisions of this Section shall result in LICENSEE losing all rights under this Agreement.

(Note that this clause requires you to have developed an FCPA company policy, which in any case is good practice.)

Source Code Escrow. An appendix with your standard source code escrow amendment and permission for the licensee to use it may suffice here. The point here is your channel partner may need to be able furnish an escrow arrangement on your behalf in order to close big sales.

Agreement

INTERNATIONAL SOFTWARE MARKETING AND LICENSE AGREEMENT

BETWEEN

VENDOR, INC.

—AND—

_____

THIS INTERNATIONAL SOFTWARE MARKETING AND LICENSE AGREEMENT is made this _____st/nd/rd/th day of _____, 19/20_____ by and between

_____, a corporation organized and existing under the laws of _____ (hereinafter referred to as "LICENSEE"), having offices at _____ .

—and—

VENDOR, INC., a corporation organized and existing under the laws of Delaware, United States of America (hereinafter referred to as "VENDOR"), having its principal office at 222 North 5th Street, Anytown, NY 00000.

For good and valuable consideration, the receipt and sufficiency of which are hereby acknowledged, it is hereby agreed as follows:

1. Definitions

    a. *"CPU"* shall mean the central processing unit of the End User's (as defined below) computer on which the Licensed Programs (as defined below) are installed.

    b. *"End User"* shall mean any user in the Territory (as defined below) who has the right to use the Licensed Programs in the Territory for its own internal business use and not for any other use, including, without limitation, remarketing, resale, relicensing, or other redistribution, either alone or as a component of any other product.

    c. *"End-User Sublicense Agreement"* shall mean an agreement entered into by an End User for the use of the Licensed Programs. Such agreement shall contain the mandatory provisions set out in Exhibit A and conform fully with the approval process described below in Section 3 before it is used by LICENSEE to sublicense the Licensed Programs to End Users.

    d. *"Intellectual Property Rights"* shall mean and include all copyrights, trademarks, trade names, intellectual property rights, and other proprietary rights or applications therefor which VENDOR may own, adapt, have the right to use or sublicense, or register with respect to the Licensed Programs or its business.

e. *"Licensed Programs"* shall mean the proprietary computer programs identified in Exhibit B, as may be amended from time to time by VENDOR in its sole discretion during the term of this Agreement. Licensed Programs will be understood to include: (i) magnetic computer tapes encoded with VENDOR's proprietary computer programs in Object Code (as defined below); (ii) all related user documentation; and (iii) any authorized copies of such items.

f. *"Maintenance and Support Services"* shall mean: (i) those reasonable efforts required by LICENSEE to maintain each Licensed Program in an operable condition in accordance with the technical specifications supplied by VENDOR; and (ii) those periodic enhancements, improvements, and corrections to the Licensed Programs as may be generally incorporated into the Licensed Programs by VENDOR (provided such are not optional features or new releases not generally made available to VENDOR's other customers without charge) and made available from time to time by VENDOR to its customers and LICENSEE, and made available by LICENSEE to End Users within the Territory.

g. *"Maintenance Agreement"* shall mean the agreement entered into between LICENSEE and its End Users whereby LICENSEE agrees to provide Maintenance and Support Services to such End Users.

h. *"Object Code"* shall mean the compiled or assembled machine language representation of a sequence of computer instructions.

i. *"Territory"* shall mean the geographic territory set forth in Exhibit C.

2. Appointment

a. VENDOR hereby grants to LICENSEE and LICENSEE accepts from VENDOR a personal, nontransferable, exclusive license solely to: (i) market and sublicense the Licensed Programs to End Users for use of the Licensed Programs in the Territory; (ii) to use the Licensed Programs solely to demonstrate the same to prospective End Users; (iii) to use the Licensed Programs to perform all LICENSEE's required installation and Maintenance and Support Services obligations under this Agreement; and (iv) to reproduce copies of the Licensed Programs in Object Code form as reasonably necessary to install, demonstrate, maintain, or support the Licensed Programs as permitted under this

Agreement and to provide such copies to End Users. Subject to the reservations provided below, LICENSEE may not appoint any sublicensees under this Agreement or sublicense the Licensed Programs to anyone other than End Users in the Territory.

b. The relationship between VENDOR and LICENSEE shall be that of independent contractor; no principal-agent, employer-employee, or similar arrangement shall exist between them, and neither party has, nor will represent it has, any power or right to, and shall not attempt to, expressly or by implication, incur any liability on behalf of the other or in any way pledge the other's credit or accept any order or make any contract binding upon the other or otherwise bind the other in any way or hold itself out as an agent or employee of the other.

c. Except with VENDOR's prior written consent, LICENSEE shall not market or sublicense the Licensed Programs to any End Users located outside the Territory. VENDOR, however, reserves the right to market and license the Licensed Programs to: (i) hardware or software original equipment manufacturers (**"OEMs"**) who in turn may market and sublicense the Licensed Programs to customers of their hardware or software products whether or not such customers are located within the Territory; and (ii) multijurisdiction end users who maintain, directly or indirectly, installations both inside and outside the Territory, where VENDOR's initial marketing contact was with such end user outside the Territory (**"Multijurisdiction End User"**). In the event that VENDOR licenses the Licensed Programs to any OEMs principally located within the Territory, VENDOR shall pay to LICENSEE an amount equal to ten percent (10%) of the Net Revenue received by VENDOR from such OEMs. For this purpose, **"Net Revenue"** will be the gross license fees received by VENDOR from such OEMs under licenses of the Licensed Programs less all charges, fees, taxes, duties, and other charges of any nature whatsoever paid or withheld from the gross license fees.

d. If, consistent with the terms of Subsection 2c above, VENDOR enters into a license agreement with a Multijurisdiction End User which involves the installation of Licensed Programs at locations both outside and within the Territory, then all Net Revenues (as defined in Subsection 2c above) received by VENDOR from such Multijurisdiction End User for use of the

Licensed Programs within the Territory shall be divided equally between VENDOR and LICENSEE. In consideration for sharing the Net Revenue received from such End Users, LICENSEE shall assume all servicing responsibility for the Licensed Programs used by such Multijurisdiction End Users in the Territory. If there is any dispute about this provision, representatives of VENDOR and LICENSEE shall meet and attempt to resolve the same in good faith.

e. At any time after the end of the second year of the term of this Agreement, provided that the Agreement is still in effect at such time, either party shall have the option to enter into an equity joint venture company with the other party for the marketing and licensing of the Licensed Programs in the Territory upon terms mutually acceptable to both parties to the extent that such an arrangement is within the laws and regulations of the Territory. The joint venture company will be organized under the laws of the Territory. Upon the establishment of the joint venture company, this Agreement will terminate without termination indemnities or other monies being owed to LICENSEE as a result of such termination and VENDOR will grant to the joint venture company the rights to market and sublicense the Licensed Programs in the Territory. Both parties agree to negotiate such joint venture in good faith.

3. End-User Sublicense Agreement

a. LICENSEE shall enter into an End-User Sublicense Agreement with each End User prior to delivery of any Licensed Programs to such End User.

b. LICENSEE may not license the Licensed Programs to End Users until LICENSEE has obtained VENDOR's prior written approval of the form of the End-User Sublicense Agreement to be used. If the End-User Sublicense Agreement is not in the English language, LICENSEE will provide VENDOR with a certified English translation of the Agreement when LICENSEE submits the form to VENDOR for its approval. LICENSEE will not modify an End-User Sublicense Agreement form previously approved by VENDOR without VENDOR's prior written approval.

c. LICENSEE shall be free to establish and alter the prices and pricing arrangements to its End Users within the Territory as it determines in its sole discretion.

4. License Fees and Taxes

    a. LICENSEE shall pay to VENDOR **"License Fees"** on each Licensed Program sublicensed to an End User pursuant to an End-User Sublicense Agreement as follows: The amount of the License Fees shall equal the total of: (i) fifty percent (50%) of the greater of (a) the total fees charged by LICENSEE to the End User for the Licensed Program (**"Sub-license Fees"**) or (b) VENDOR's then-current U.S. price list for the applicable Licensed Program(s); (ii) fifty percent (50%) of the greater of (a) the maintenance fees charged by LICENSEE to the End User for Maintenance of the Licensed Program (**"Sublicense Maintenance Fees"**), or (b) the applicable Maintenance Fee for the relevant Licensed Program(s) as stated in the then-current VENDOR U.S. price list; and (iii) any taxes, duties, or charges of any nature required to be made or paid for payments due to VENDOR under (i) and (ii) above except for withholding taxes imposed by the laws of the Territory on VENDOR's income. In the case of any such withholding, LICENSEE shall furnish VENDOR with official tax receipts or other evidence of payment issued by the taxing authorities of the Territory.

    b. If LICENSEE enters into a multiyear Maintenance Agreement for any of the Licensed Programs (whether or not prepaid) with any End User, the Sublicense and Sublicense Maintenance Fees for purposes of (ii)(a) of Subsection 4a above shall be based on the total amount payable during the entire contract period and shall be considered to have been received by LICENSEE during the month such Maintenance Agreement is signed by the End User.

    c. Upon the signing of this Agreement, LICENSEE shall pay to VENDOR U.S. $ _____ as an advance payment of monies and License Fees owed LICENSEE to VENDOR under this Agreement.

    d. LICENSEE shall give notification by telefax to VENDOR (followed by confirmation copy sent via airmail, together with a copy of each such agreement) of each End-User Sublicense Agreement and Maintenance Agreement no later than the 5th day of the month following the month in which such agreements are executed, or the month when the Licensed Program(s) are delivered by LICENSEE to the End User, whichever shall first occur. Such notice shall specify, at a minimum, the Licensed Program(s) involved; the End-User's CPU model and serial number; the name, address, and telephone number of the End User; and the Sublicense Fees and Sublicense Maintenance Fees charged by LICENSEE to the End User stated in the currency of the Territory. LICENSEE shall pay all License Fees to VENDOR within thirty (30) calendar days after its receipt of the Sublicense Fees and Maintenance Fees from the End Users (with pro ration of all partial payments), but in no event later than ninety (90) calendar days from the date the End-User Sublicense Agreement is signed, or Licensed Program installation at End-User site, whichever is earlier. All License Fees shall be due and payable to VENDOR in United States dollars (based as applicable on the exchange rate quoted in *The Wall Street Journal* at the time the End-User Agreement is signed), either by wire transfer or by deposit in such account or with such third party as VENDOR shall direct in writing from time to time.

e. If any government shall impose restrictions upon the amount or manner of any remittances to VENDOR under this Agreement, VENDOR may, in its sole discretion, elect either to terminate the Agreement pursuant to the provisions of Section 13 hereof or to accept payment in any other manner which may be lawfully available. LICENSEE will cooperate with VENDOR and make every reasonable effort requested by VENDOR, at VENDOR's expense, to obtain any necessary or expedient governmental approval for the payments specified in this Agreement. Until such remittance can lawfully be made, funds representing any excess of the payments due hereunder over and above such part thereof as can be lawfully remitted shall be held in the country in question in U.S. currency (after conversion), if possible, and if not in local currency, upon trust and for the account of VENDOR earning the best possible interest as appropriate to investments of this nature. VENDOR may, if it thinks fit and to the extent permitted by applicable law, require the LICENSEE to make payments to a specified corporation or bank and payment in accordance with the said requirements shall constitute payment of such monies to VENDOR and the LICENSEE shall accordingly be released from any further obligation in connection therewith.

f. If the total Sublicense Fees and Sublicense Maintenance Fees received by the LICENSEE during any Quota Year (as defined in Section 13) have exceeded the Revenue Quota (as defined in Exhibit D), then the percentage given in (i) of Subsection 4a above shall be reduced to forty percent (40%) for all subsequent Sublicense Fees obtained for the remainder of that Quota Year. If LICENSEE enters into an End-User Sublicense Agreement for a term that is not specified in VENDOR's then-current U.S. price list, the price to be used for purposes of (i) (b) of Subsection 4a above shall be VENDOR's then-current U.S. 99-year license price.

5. Training; Materials; Assistance

    a. Upon execution of this Agreement, at the LICENSEE's expense, VENDOR will provide training to the initial technical and sales personnel of LICENSEE on such reasonable schedule as shall be determined by LICENSEE and VENDOR. Upon the request of LICENSEE and at LICENSEE's sole expense, VENDOR may from time to time, during the term of this Agreement, make available to LICENSEE's personnel additional training programs. Any such training shall be conducted in English, subject to the availability of VENDOR personnel. VENDOR will separately invoice the LICENSEE for the cost of such training, which amount shall be payable by LICENSEE within thirty (30) calendar days from receipt of the invoice. LICENSEE shall bear all incidental costs incurred in connection with all such training including, without limitation, transportation, lodging, and meals.

    b. In addition to the training provided for in Subsection 5a above, VENDOR shall undertake from time to time during the term of this Agreement and subject to the availability of VENDOR personnel, at the request and sole expense of LICENSEE, to render to LICENSEE in English such reasonable commercial and technical assistance in connection with LICENSEE's support and marketing of the Licensed Programs, including sending VENDOR personnel to the Territory to assist the LICENSEE with the marketing of the Licensed Programs. VENDOR will separately invoice the LICENSEE for the cost of such assistance, which amount shall be payable by LICENSEE within thirty (30) calendar days from receipt of the invoice. The LICENSEE will also be responsible for all costs incurred by VENDOR personnel in connection with such assistance, including, without limitation, all travel, meals, and lodging costs.

c. LICENSEE may offer training programs on the use of the Licensed Programs to the End Users, provided such training is consistent with the training given by VENDOR to its customers and is done by qualified personnel of LICENSEE who have successfully completed the training program offered hereunder by VENDOR. All costs of such training shall be borne by LICENSEE, who shall also be entitled to all revenue therefrom. Such revenue will not be included for purposes of the Revenue Quotas described in Exhibit D hereto.

d. At LICENSEE's request, VENDOR shall, where appropriate, issue to LICENSEE such reasonable numbers of copies in English of available sales brochures and manuals as they become available (**"Sales Materials"**). Such materials shall be provided to LICENSEE at the prices shown on VENDOR's then-current Licensee's Price List. One copy of each updated manual will also be provided without charge at each new release of the Licensed Programs for each customer currently under a Maintenance Agreement.

e. VENDOR shall deliver to LICENSEE a master distribution tape or diskette containing the Object Code for the Licensed Programs, and thereafter, as appropriate under this Agreement, shall similarly deliver a replacement master distribution tape or diskette containing the Object Code for the Licensed Program whenever VENDOR generally releases a modified or updated version thereof. Nothing in this provision or Agreement shall entitle LICENSEE to receive the source code or any portion thereof of the Licensed Programs. LICENSEE may make distribution copies of the Licensed Programs from these masters, always affixing the tape label supplied or approved by VENDOR to the copies. VENDOR will further deliver to LICENSEE the following material for LICENSEE's use consistent with the terms of this Agreement, and LICENSEE agrees to be responsible for complying with all applicable laws respecting the proprietary and confidential nature of the materials in the Territory:

- five (5) copies of the available documentation in English for the Licensed Programs;

- five (5) copies of existing current sales material in English for the Licensed Programs;

- five (5) copies of updates of documentation as VENDOR makes such generally available; and

- Licensed Program technical fixes as they are made generally available by VENDOR, or periodically, at the sole and exclusive option of VENDOR.

f. LICENSEE shall pay all costs of shipping and applicable taxes, duties, and other charges relating to bulk shipments of materials ordered by and delivered to LICENSEE under this Agreement. All materials sent to LICENSEE shall be sent to its notice address as specified in Section 16 hereof. VENDOR may either send or deliver COD or invoice LICENSEE for such costs. LICENSEE shall be responsible for obtaining, at LICENSEE's cost, all necessary governmental approvals, permits, and licenses in connection with the shipment and importation of the Licensed Programs and other materials mentioned in Subsection 5e above and shall be solely responsible for the payment of any duties, taxes, or other governmental changes imposed upon importation of such items into the Territory.

6. Changes and Developments

VENDOR reserves the exclusive right to change the Licensed Programs or any related technical or marketing materials at any time and from time to time in its sole discretion. VENDOR agrees to keep the LICENSEE informed of and issue the LICENSEE as part of the Licensed Programs all corrections to the Licensed Programs as soon as the same are made generally available by VENDOR. Changes to the Licensed Programs by VENDOR, including any revised or additional support or training materials, will be made available to LICENSEE for marketing and sublicensing as part of the Licensed Programs when and as VENDOR determines to make them generally available to its licensees. LICENSEE shall have no right to change, modify, merge, package for licensing with other products, or otherwise to market or deal with the Licensed Programs except as expressly provided in this Agreement.

7. Maintenance and Support Services; Conversion

a. During the term of this Agreement, LICENSEE agrees to employ no fewer than _____ technical and support personnel who will work exclusively and on a full-time basis in connection with its marketing and the Maintenance and Support Services. In fulfilling its Maintenance and Support Services, LICENSEE shall provide all End Users with the following services:

  i. Prompt response to, analysis and handling of all assistance, needs, and requests in connection with the Maintenance and Support Services;

  ii. An efficient and effective call control facility to deal with such assistance, needs, and requests and to perform its other duties under this Agreement relating to the Licensed Programs and an efficient and effective support staff sufficiently widespread throughout the Territory to respond promptly to such calls; and

  iii. Prompt replacement of any corrupted or damaged copy of any Licensed Programs.

b. During the continuance of this Agreement, VENDOR shall have the responsibility, at VENDOR's expense, to respond to, or cause to be responded to, all Licensed Program assistance, maintenance, and support needs and requests involving a failure of the Licensed Programs to operate in accordance with the then-current and published VENDOR Licensed Program specifications in a fashion which, in the opinion of VENDOR, requires correction or modification of the Licensed Programs (**"Technical Failures"**). All Technical Failures shall be referred by LICENSEE immediately to VENDOR for maintenance service by VENDOR. LICENSEE shall cooperate in all reasonable respects with VENDOR in attempting to resolve all Technical Failures. VENDOR will exercise reasonable efforts to correct any Technical Failures, but does not represent that none exist or that if they do, they can be remedied.

c. LICENSEE shall not translate or adapt the Licensed Programs or the Sales Materials in any way without VENDOR's prior written consent. In the event that VENDOR gives its consent, VENDOR and LICENSEE shall enter into separate translation or adaptation agreements. All such adaptation and translation work must be performed by LICENSEE's technicians or employees at a mutually agreed location. LICENSEE shall be responsible for all expenses related to such adaptation or translation. In the separate translation or adaptation agreements, the parties shall agree, among other items, that VENDOR shall retain all rights in the translated or adapted work, including without limitation, copyrights. In such agreements,

LICENSEE shall irrevocably assign to VENDOR all rights, interests, and title it might have in the translation or adaptation and agrees to execute all documents required under the law of the Territory in order to effect such assignment. VENDOR reserves the right to review and approve all such translations or adaptations. In no event, however, shall VENDOR be liable to any party due to errors made in the translations or adaptations, and LICENSEE agrees to indemnify and hold VENDOR harmless from and against all damages, losses, injuries, or expenses (including attorneys' fees) resulting from an error in such translations or adaptations.

8. Undertakings by the LICENSEE

LICENSEE undertakes and agrees with VENDOR that it:

a. represents and warrants that it has, and will maintain during the terms of this Agreement, substantial expertise, qualified personnel, and capacity to perform its obligations hereunder;

b. will use at all times all reasonable endeavors to promote and extend the market for the Licensed Programs to all potential End Users in the Territory and work no less diligently to obtain orders therefor than for any other products distributed or marketed by LICENSEE; LICENSEE will provide its salespeople incentives to promote the Licensed Programs which equal or exceed the incentives provided to them to promote any other products distributed by LICENSEE. LICENSEE agrees to permit VENDOR to provide LICENSEE's personnel additional incentives from time to time relating to special VENDOR sales campaigns;

c. will at its own expense provide advertising and publicity in the Territory for the Licensed Programs at least as extensive as the advertising and publicity provided by the LICENSEE for other products which it distributes or markets in the Territory except in those cases where the LICENSEE is involved in a cooperative advertising program in which case the portion contributed by a third party to LICENSEE's publicity for such other products will be excluded from the above calculation. LICENSEE shall, prior to use of any publicity or advertising of the Licensed Programs, submit all such materials, together with English translations thereof if in a language other than English, to VENDOR for its written approval, which approval shall be

deemed to be given if no disapproval is received from VEN-
DOR within ten (10) calendar days of VENDOR's receipt of
such submissions from the LICENSEE;

d. will not without the previous written consent of VENDOR,
either directly or indirectly develop, produce, import, market,
sell, license, sublicense, rent, promote, or advertise any software which, in the opinion of VENDOR, is so like or similar to
the Licensed Programs as to be capable of competing with the
Licensed Programs;

e. will in all correspondence and other dealings related directly or
indirectly to the sublicensing or other transactions relating to
the Licensed Programs clearly indicate that it is acting as
licensee and not as author, developer, or owner of the Licensed
Programs;

f. will not at any time, including after termination hereof, incur
or purport to incur any liability on behalf of VENDOR or in
any way pledge or purport to pledge VENDOR's credit or
purport to make any contract binding upon VENDOR;

g. will permit any duly authorized representative of VENDOR to
enter, during normal business hours, into any of its premises
where any Licensed Programs or any materials relating thereto
are located for the purpose of ascertaining that the provisions
of this Agreement are being complied with by the LICENSEE;

h. will at all times promptly bring to the attention of VENDOR any
information received by the LICENSEE which is likely to be
of interest, use, or benefit to VENDOR in relation to the marketing and/or support of the Licensed Programs, except for
such information that LICENSEE receives under a legal
obligation of nondisclosure;

i. will at all times, including after termination hereof, keep full,
proper, and up-to-date books of account and records showing
clearly all inquiries, transactions, proceedings, maintenance
and service calls relating to the Licensed Programs and this
Agreement generally, and will allow any duly authorized representative of VENDOR to have reasonable access to and to
audit said books and records, and take such copies thereof at
VENDOR's expense, as such representative may reasonably
require;

j. will provide detailed monthly and annual reports in English,
including copies of all End-User Sublicense Agreements, Maintenance Agreements, payments, and License Fees, rolling 30-,

60-, and 90-day nonbinding good faith business forecast reports on forms provided by or acceptable to VENDOR, and from time to time supply to VENDOR such other reports and information relating to this Agreement as VENDOR may reasonably request, the annual report to include the following year's marketing plan and to be certified as accurate by the financial officer of LICENSEE; monthly reports shall be provided to VENDOR within five (5) calendar days of the end of the period which is being reported; the annual report to be provided within thirty (30) calendar days after the end of the contract year; these reports shall include the U.S. dollar equivalent of all Sublicense and Sublicense Maintenance Fees received by LICENSEE from End Users during each month, converted into U.S. dollars at the official exchange rate quoted in *The Wall Street Journal* on the date of the End-User Sublicense Agreement was signed by both parties and shall include a year-to-date U.S. dollar equivalent amount;

k. will at all times, including after termination hereof, if reasonably requested, join with VENDOR, and otherwise fully cooperate with VENDOR, at the expense of VENDOR, in any proceedings necessary for the protection of Intellectual Property Rights in the Licensed Programs and will give notice to VENDOR forthwith of any circumstances coming to the knowledge of the LICENSEE which might indicate an infringement of such rights;

l. acknowledges that all Licensed Programs and all documents, information, and materials related to such Licensed Programs and Maintenance (hereafter, such Licensed Programs, and related documents, information, and materials shall be referred to collectively as **"Technical Data"**) are subject to United States export controls pursuant to the Export Administration Regulations, 15 CFR Parts 740-799. At all times LICENSEE shall comply strictly with all requirements of the Export Administration Regulations and all licenses and authorizations issued thereunder with respect to all such Technical Data. In furtherance of the foregoing obligation, LICENSEE agrees that, without the prior written authorization of VENDOR and the United States Commerce Department, LICENSEE will not, and will cause its representatives and customers to agree not to, (i) directly or indirectly export, re-export, divert, or transfer any of the Technical Data, or any direct product thereof from the Territory, or (ii) directly or indirectly disclose any Technical Data to any individual or entity not a national of the Territory. LICENSEE shall make records available to VENDOR, at VENDOR's reasonable request, in order to permit VENDOR to confirm LICENSEE's compliance with its obligations as set forth in this Subsection (l). The obligations set forth in this Subsection (l) shall survive termination of this Agreement, regardless of the cause or absence of cause therefor;

m. represents and warrants as to all Licensed Programs that nothing in this Agreement violates any applicable law or regulation or contract or agreement to which LICENSEE is a party or to which it is subject, that this Agreement is enforceable in accordance with its terms and acknowledges that VENDOR has entered into this Agreement expressly in reliance on the representations and warranties by LICENSEE;

n. will have full responsibility at LICENSEE's expense for compliance with all laws applicable to LICENSEE's operations, to this Agreement and all sublicense and other agreements (including timely payment of all fees, taxes, duties, or other charges payable by LICENSEE), and shall obtain all approvals, consents, or permits required in connection with the same, and LICENSEE will immediately inform VENDOR of all such requirements and provide copies to VENDOR of all information, documentation, and correspondence concerning the same;

o. will comply with any requests reasonably made by VENDOR in relation to the marketing, sublicensing, or maintenance of the Licensed Programs, and ensure that the Licensed Programs as marketed and sold shall not be of lesser quality than those produced and supplied by VENDOR;

p. will maintain and support the existing customers of VENDOR in the Territory as listed in Exhibit E during the term of this Agreement; and

q. will provide VENDOR with copies of all documents relating to any amount withheld by government authority on License Fees and other payments made or due to VENDOR.

LICENSEE SHALL INDEMNIFY AND HOLD VENDOR HARMLESS FROM ALL CLAIMS, DAMAGES, LOST PROFITS, COSTS, OR EXPENSES WHETHER FORESEEABLE OR UNFORESEEABLE (INCLUDING REASONABLE ATTORNEYS' FEES) ARISING FROM OR RELATED TO SUCH LICENSEE'S OPERATIONS OR ACTIVITIES OR FROM LICENSEE'S BREACH OF THIS AGREEMENT

OR ANY WARRANTY OR REPRESENTATION THAT LICENSEE MAY MAKE IN ADDITION TO OR IN LIEU OF THOSE SPECIFICALLY GRANTED BY VENDOR WITH RESPECT TO THE Licensed Programs.

9. Undertakings by VENDOR

VENDOR undertakes and agrees with LICENSEE that it will at all times during the continuance in force of this Agreement, and where applicable following termination hereof, observe and perform the terms and conditions set out in this Agreement and in particular:

    a. pass to the LICENSEE all leads or inquiries relating to the Licensed Programs that it may receive from potential End Users within the Territory;

    b. respond to requests from the LICENSEE for support in accordance with Section 7b above, and for such purpose to maintain suitably qualified staff to provide efficient and effective support thereunder;

    c. give to the LICENSEE notice of any Licensed Program enhancement, upgrade, modification, variation, suspension or elimination, in accordance with Section 7 above;

    d. promptly make available to LICENSEE as it becomes available to VENDOR all information including market information relating to the Licensed Programs which VENDOR reasonably considers to be important to LICENSEE; and

    e. represent and warrant that it has not conveyed title to the Licensed Programs to any other person.

VENDOR SHALL INDEMNIFY AND HOLD LICENSEE HARMLESS FROM ALL CLAIMS, DAMAGES, LOSSES, COSTS, OR EXPENSES (INCLUDING REASONABLE ATTORNEYS' FEES) ARISING FROM OR RELATING TO VENDOR'S MATERIAL BREACH OF THE AGREEMENT.

10. Limited Warranty

    a. In addition to the limited warranty regarding Technical Failures in Section 7b hereof, VENDOR warrants only that, upon delivery to LICENSEE and for a period of ninety (90) calendar days thereafter, each master distribution tape of the Licensed Programs will operate substantially in accordance with the accompanying documentation. In case of breach of this limited warranty or any other duty that relates to the quality of the master distribution tape, LICENSEE's exclusive remedies will be, at VENDOR's option: (i) correction of the master distribution tape; (ii) replacement of the master distribution tape; or (iii) return of the master distribution tape with reimbursement to the LICENSEE of the LICENSEE Fees paid by the LICENSEE to VENDOR during this warranty period for Licensed Programs copied from such master distribution tape.

b. EXCEPT AS EXPRESSLY PROVIDED ABOVE, ALL WARRANTIES, CONDITIONS, REPRESENTATIONS, INDEMNITIES, AND GUARANTEES, WHETHER EXPRESS OR IMPLIED, ARISING BY LAW, CUSTOM, PRIOR ORAL OR WRITTEN STATEMENTS BY VENDOR OR OTHERWISE (INCLUDING, BUT NOT LIMITED TO, ANY WARRANTY OR MERCHANTABILITY OR FITNESS FOR PARTICULAR PURPOSES OR OF ERROR-FREE AND UNINTERRUPTED USE) ARE HEREBY OVERRIDDEN, EXCLUDED, AND DISCLAIMED.

c. UNDER NO CIRCUMSTANCES WILL VENDOR OR ITS RELATED COMPANIES BE LIABLE FOR ANY CONSEQUENTIAL, INDIRECT, OR SPECIAL DAMAGES, WHETHER FORESEEABLE OR UNFORESEEABLE, BASED ON CLAIMS OF LICENSEE OR ITS End Users (INCLUDING, BUT NOT LIMITED TO, CLAIMS FOR LOSS OF DATA, GOODWILL, PROFITS, USE OF MONEY, OR USE OF THE Licensed Programs, INTERRUPTION IN USE OR AVAILABILITY OF DATA OR PROGRAMS, INTERRUPTION IN USE OR AVAILABILITY OF DATA OR THE Licensed Programs, STOPPAGE OR OTHER WORK OR IMPAIRMENT OF OTHER ASSETS), ARISING OUT OF BREACH OF EXPRESS OR IMPLIED WARRANTY, BREACH OF CONTRACT, MISREPRESENTATION, NEGLIGENCE, STRICT LIABILITY IN TORT OR OTHERWISE, EXCEPT ONLY IN THE CASE OF PERSONAL INJURY WHERE AND TO THE EXTENT THAT APPLICABLE LAW REQUIRES SUCH LIABILITY. IN NO EVENT WILL THE AGGREGATE LIABILITY WHICH VENDOR AND ITS RELATED COMPANIES MUST INCUR IN ANY ACTION OR PROCEEDING

EXCEED THE TOTAL AMOUNT ACTUALLY PAID TO VENDOR FOR OR IN CONNECTION WITH THE PARTICULAR Licensed Program THAT DIRECTLY CAUSED THE DAMAGE.

11. Intellectual Property Rights

a. LICENSEE acknowledges that any and all Intellectual Property Rights used or embodied in or in connection with the Licensed Programs, including all documentation and manuals relating thereto, all translations, conversions, and adaptations made by LICENSEE to the Licensed Programs, are and shall remain the exclusive property of VENDOR and LICENSEE shall not, during or at any time after the expiration or termination of this Agreement, take any action which would jeopardize VENDOR's proprietary rights in the Licensed Programs.

b. LICENSEE acknowledges and agrees that the Licensed Programs (including methods, processes, or techniques utilized in the Licensed Programs) are proprietary to and valuable trade secrets of VENDOR and LICENSEE agrees to maintain their confidential nature by exercising at least the same degree of care to protect the confidentiality of the Licensed Programs as it would exercise in protecting its own most sensitive confidential information. LICENSEE agrees that it will take all reasonable steps necessary to ensure that the Licensed Programs shall not be disclosed to, or used by or for the benefit of, any person, association, or entity except permitted End Users of LICENSEE and LICENSEE's employees (all of whom shall also first execute confidentiality agreements of the form attached to this Agreement as Exhibit F) as strictly necessary for performance of LICENSEE's obligations under this Agreement. LICENSEE agrees not to remove or destroy any eye-readable or machine-readable proprietary markings or confidentiality legends or other references to VENDOR as author or developer or to its rights in the Licensed Programs placed upon or contained within the Licensed Programs and shall copy the same on all permitted copies in both English and the language of the Territory. In no event shall LICENSEE cause or permit the reverse engineering, disassembly, decompiling, customizing, transferring, downloading, merging, or otherwise modification of a Licensed Program without the prior written consent of VENDOR. Except as expressly authorized under Section 2 above, LICENSEE shall not otherwise use, copy, modify, transfer, or otherwise deal with the Licensed Programs.

c. LICENSEE also acknowledges that such rights belonging to VENDOR are used only by LICENSEE with the consent of VENDOR to the extent expressly provided in and during continuation of this Agreement. Upon expiry or termination hereof, the LICENSEE shall forthwith discontinue such use without receipt of compensation for such discontinuance. Upon termination or expiry hereof, LICENSEE shall immediately return all Licensed Programs and copies thereof, support materials and other materials or information provided by VENDOR or relating to this Agreement or the Licensed Programs and shall promptly certify to VENDOR as to such return.

d. LICENSEE is hereby granted a nonexclusive license, during the term of this Agreement only, to use the name "VENDOR" and those trademarks listed in Exhibit B solely to the extent required and for the purposes of performing its obligations under this Agreement. The form of any such uses shall be first approved by VENDOR. LICENSEE shall not during or after the expiry or termination of this Agreement without the prior written consent of VENDOR use or adopt any trade name, trademark, trading style, or commercial designation that includes or is similar to or may be mistaken for the whole or any part of any trademark, trade name, trading style, or commercial designation used by VENDOR. At VENDOR's request and expense, LICENSEE will assist VENDOR in registration in the Territory of its trademarks and copyrights.

e. If LICENSEE believes that any third party is infringing VENDOR's Intellectual Property Rights or is committing any action which amounts to passing off its trade as that of VENDOR, LICENSEE shall immediately notify VENDOR who may at its sole discretion prosecute such infringer. LICENSEE will in the performance of its duties under this Agreement use all reasonable efforts to safeguard the property rights and interest of VENDOR and will at the request and cost of VENDOR take all steps reasonably required by VENDOR to defend such rights.

f. If any claim made against LICENSEE that the use or possession of the Licensed Programs infringes any patent, copyright, or like Intellectual Property Right, the LICENSEE shall immediately notify VENDOR who may at its sole discretion defend such claim. LICENSEE shall have no right to make any demands or claims, bring suit, effect any settlement, or take any other action in respect of the Licensed Programs without the prior written consent of VENDOR.

g. LICENSEE agrees to indemnify and hold VENDOR harmless against all damages and losses (including reasonable attorneys' fees) resulting from LICENSEE's failure to protect VENDOR's rights and interests in the Licensed Programs as required under this Agreement.

12. *Force Majeure*

Neither party shall be under any liability to the other or to any other party in any way whatsoever for destruction, damage, delay, or any other matters of any nature whatsoever arising out of war, rebellion, civil commotion, strikes, lockouts and industrial disputes, fire, explosion, earthquake, act of God, flood or bad weather, the unavailability of deliveries, supplies, software, Licensed Programs, discs, tapes or other media or the requisitioning or other act or order by any government, department, council, or other constituted body or other matter outside of that party's reasonable control. If such an event shall continue for more than sixty (60) consecutive calendar days or for a total period of ninety (90) calendar days during any period of twelve (12) consecutive months, either party may immediately terminate this Agreement. In no event, however, shall such an event excuse LICENSEE from its obligations of confidentiality and to make payments to VENDOR which accrued prior to the occurrence of such an event.

13. *Term, Termination or Expiration, Consequences of Termination*

a. This Agreement shall take effect as of the date indicated above when signed by both parties (the **"Commencement Date"**) and shall remain in effect for a period ending on _____ (the **"Initial Term"**) unless earlier terminated pursuant to Subsections 13b through 13e below. The Initial Term hereof shall be extended automatically for additional periods of one (1) year each (**"Subsequent Terms"**) unless either party shall, at least ninety (90) calendar days prior to the expiration of the Initial Term or any of the subsequent Terms, give written notice to the other of its intent to terminate the Agreement at the end of such term. Notwithstanding any successive renewals hereunder, this Agreement shall be considered for all purposes a definite term agreement and not an indefinite term agreement. This Agreement shall remain wholly executory until the issuance of all government approvals required by the laws of the Territory. If such government approvals are not received within two months of the Commencement Date, this Agreement shall be deemed null and void.

b. This Agreement may be terminated by VENDOR without administrative or judicial resolution without cost to VENDOR and in its sole discretion, as to all Licensed Programs and the entire Territory, if during any **"Quota Year"** (each Quota Year under this Agreement being a successive 12-month period, the first 12-month period commencing on the Commencement Date of this Agreement), the total revenues derived by LICENSEE from Sublicense Fees (exclusive of taxes, duties, and other charges) for which applicable License Fees have been received by VENDOR are less than the Revenue Quotas shown or determined on or pursuant to Exhibit D. If the Revenue Quotas are not met for the applicable period, VENDOR may terminate this Agreement at any time during sixty (60) calendar days following receipt from the LICENSEE of the annual report as provided for in Section 8i hereof or following the period when such report should have been made by giving written notice to LICENSEE of such termination.

c. Notwithstanding any provisions herein contained this Agreement may be terminated immediately without administrative or judicial resolution by notice in writing from the party not at fault if any of the following events shall occur:

    i. if the other party fails to pay any outstanding amounts as they fall due under the terms of this Agreement;

    ii. if the other party shall commit any act of bankruptcy, shall have a receiving order or administration order made against it, shall make or negotiate for any general composition or arrangement with general assignment for the benefit of its creditors, shall present a petition or have a petition presented by a creditor for its winding up or shall enter into any liquidation, shall call any general meeting of its creditors, shall have a receiver or administrator appointed over all or any of its undertakings or assets, shall be unable generally to pay its debts or shall cease to carry on business; or

   iii. if the other party shall at any time be in default under this Agreement and shall fail to remedy such default within thirty (30) calendar days from receipt of notice in writing from the first party specifying such default.

d. VENDOR shall additionally be entitled to terminate this Agreement immediately without administrative or judicial resolution (except in the case of (ii) below) with no payment to LICENSEE upon written notice to LICENSEE: (i) if LICENSEE is a party to any merger or acquisition in which a controlling interest or all or substantially all of LICENSEE's or the business of its controlling person(s) is transferred or disposed of to any person, firm or corporation who, in the opinion of VENDOR, has interests contrary to the best interests of VENDOR or if LICENSEE includes as members of its Board of Directors or management individuals, who, in the opinion of VENDOR, have interests contrary to the best interests of VENDOR; LICENSEE shall immediately notify VENDOR in writing if it is a party to any merger or acquisition in which controlling interest in LICENSEE or its controlling persons is transferred or disposed of; or (ii) if LICENSEE is prohibited (whether by judicial or administrative order, by any contract to which LICENSEE is a party or to which it is subject, or by operation of law) from discharging its obligations hereunder. For purposes of this provision, "controlling interest" or "controlling person(s)" shall mean any interest or person(s) who, directly or indirectly either singularly or collectively, own more than ten percent (10%) of the LICENSEE. In the case of (ii) above, termination shall be effective thirty (30) calendar days after written notice unless LICENSEE shall have completely eliminated, to VENDOR's satisfaction, the prohibition which was the subject of said notice.

e. Without affecting VENDOR's rights to terminate this Agreement pursuant to Sections 13a through 13d, VENDOR shall at any time during the term of this Agreement have the right with or without cause or reason to terminate immediately this Agreement upon written notice to LICENSEE and upon the

payment to the LICENSEE of the greater of U.S. $ _____
or fifty percent (50%) of the total Sublicense Fees and Sublicense Maintenance Fees received by the LICENSEE during
the twelve (12) months immediately preceding the notice of
termination.

f. Upon the expiration or termination of this Agreement in accordance with this Section, LICENSEE will not be entitled under
law or otherwise to receive any payment from VENDOR for
actual, consequential, indirect, special or incidental damages,
costs or expenses, whether foreseeable or unforeseeable
(including, but not limited to, labor claims and loss of profits,
investments or goodwill), any right to which LICENSEE
hereby waives and disclaims to the fullest extent permitted by
law.

g. Upon any expiration or termination of this Agreement, VEN-
DOR or a third party designated by VENDOR will assume all
invoicing and collection of payments under all existing End-
User Sublicense Agreements, all amounts received by either
party after the date of termination shall be the exclusive property of VENDOR (provided that amounts in respect of payments due before the date of termination shall be apportioned
up to the date of termination), LICENSEE shall immediately
pay all amounts due to or on behalf of VENDOR, and
LICENSEE shall have no further rights under this Agreement.
All valid End-User Sublicense Agreements in existence as of
the date of termination shall survive such termination. At VEN-
DOR's election, VENDOR or a third party designated by VEN-
DOR shall receive and assume by assignment from LICENSEE
all rights and obligations of LICENSEE to the End Users under
any End-User Sublicense Agreements in force at the time of
any termination hereof. LICENSEE shall use its best efforts to
obtain, to the extent required by the laws of the Territory, the
consent of each End User to the LICENSEE's assignment of
the End-User Sublicense Agreements to VENDOR or its
designee. No termination of this Agreement shall release any
right or remedy which either party may have for any default
existing, or arising from facts or circumstances existing on the
date of termination. Any termination of this Agreement, unless
expressly stated otherwise in the notice of termination, shall be
a termination for the entire Territory and all Licensed Programs. In addition to provisions which by their express terms

shall continue after termination, all obligations under Sections 7 and 8 as applicable to post-termination claims, and Section 10 shall survive any termination of this Agreement.

If any such event referred to in this Section shall occur, termination shall become effective upon notice or on such other later date set forth in the notice.

14. Waiver

Failure or neglect by either party to enforce at any time any of the provisions hereof shall not be construed nor shall be deemed to be a waiver of such party's rights hereunder nor in any way effect the validity of the whole or any part of this Agreement nor prejudice such party's rights to take subsequent action.

15. Assignment

Neither this Agreement nor any right or obligation arising hereunder shall be assigned or transferred by the LICENSEE, whether voluntarily or involuntarily (whether by operation of law or otherwise), in whole or in part, to any party without the prior written consent of VENDOR. Any attempted assignment or transfer shall be void and of no effect. VENDOR shall have the right, in such event and in addition to any other remedy available at law or in equity, immediately to terminate this Agreement upon notice to LICENSEE. This Agreement shall not be assigned or transferred by VENDOR without prior written consent of LICENSEE unless the assignee has agreed in writing for the benefit of LICENSEE to assume all of VENDOR's obligations hereunder, provided that nothing shall prohibit VENDOR from assigning its rights and benefits hereunder, or transferring this Agreement in connection with the sale or other disposition of all or substantially all of its business in a Licensed Program or Licensed Programs.

16. Notices and Requests

Unless otherwise specifically provided, all notices required or permitted by this Agreement shall be in writing and may be delivered personally with written acknowledgment of receipt; or may be sent by facsimile with a confirming copy sent by registered airmail; or by registered airmail, postage prepaid, and return receipt requested, addressed as follows:

For LICENSEE:

For VENDOR: Vendor, Inc.
222 North 5th Street
Anytown, NY 00000
United States of America

Attn: Vice President
International

Telefax: +1 (999) 999-9999

The parties may change their addresses from time to time by giving written notice to the other party. Any notice shall be deemed to have been received as follows: (i) personal delivery and airmail upon receipt; and (ii) facsimile the day sent. Nothing contained herein shall justify or excuse failure to give oral notice for the purpose of informing the other party thereof when prompt notification is appropriate, but such oral notice shall not satisfy the requirement of written notice.

17. Governing Law and Jurisdiction

The validity, construction, and performance of this Agreement and legal relations between the parties to this Agreement shall be governed and construed in accordance with the laws of the State of New York, United States of America, excluding that body of law applicable to conflicts of law and excluding the United Nations Convention on Contracts for the International Sale of Goods, if applicable. The parties consent and submit to the exclusive jurisdiction and venue of the State and Federal Courts located in Suffolk County, New York to determine the validity, construction, and performance of this Agreement and the legal relations between the parties. Nothing in this Section will prevent VENDOR from seeking injunctive relief against the LICENSEE from any judicial or administrative authority in the Territory.

18. Attorneys Fees

If suit is brought (or arbitration instituted) or an attorney is retained by any party to this Agreement to enforce the terms of this Agreement or to collect any money due hereunder, or to collect money damages for breach hereof, the prevailing party shall be entitled to recover, in addition to any other remedy, reimbursement for reasonable attorneys' fees, court costs, costs of investigation, and other related expenses incurred in connection therewith as determined by a court.

19. Severability

To the fullest extent possible each provision of this Agreement shall be interpreted in such fashion as to be effective and valid under applicable law. If any provision of this Agreement is declared void or unenforceable under particular circumstances, such provision shall remain in full force and effect in all other circumstances. If any provision of this Agreement is declared totally void or unenforceable, such provision shall be deemed severed from this Agreement which shall otherwise remain in full force and effect. If any such modification of this Agreement pursuant to this Section shall materially affect the economic benefits or viability of this Agreement to either party, this Agreement may be terminated by either party upon notice to the other party.

20. Interest

To the extent any amount becomes due and owing hereunder, the party to whom such amount is payable shall be entitled to receive, in addition to such amount, interest thereon at the rate of two percent (2%) per month (or such lower rate as shall be the highest permissible contract rate under applicable law) from and after the date the amount was due.

21. Entire Agreement; Amendment

This Agreement (which shall include all Exhibits attached or delivered pursuant hereto) represents the complete and exclusive statement of the agreements between the parties relating to the subject matter and there are no warranties, representations, or agreements between them relating to such subject matter except as set forth in this Agreement.

IN WITNESS whereof the parties hereto have caused two (2) original copies of this Agreement to be signed for the same effect and purpose.

VENDOR, Inc.

————————————
"LICENSEE"

By: ————————————
       President

By: ————————————

————————————

Date: ————————————

Date: ————————————

EXHIBIT A
TO
INTERNATIONAL SOFTWARE MARKETING
AND LICENSE AGREEMENT

MANDATORY PROVISIONS
FOR END-USER SUBLICENSE AGREEMENT

1. Sublicense

Sublicensor grants a personal, nontransferable and nonexclusive right to use the Licensed Programs on the CPU specified below during this term of the End-User Sublicense Agreement.

CPU Identification Number	Description	Location

2. Licensed Programs

"Licensed Programs" shall mean the proprietary computer programs identified in Exhibit A. Licensed Programs will be understood to include: (i) computer magnetic tapes encoded with VENDOR's proprietary computer programs in Object Code (as defined below); (ii) all related user documentation; and (iii) all copies of such items.

3. Use

End User may use Licensed Programs only for its own internal business use and only on the CPU and at the location designated above. End User will not permit any other person to use the Licensed Programs. End User may make one (1) back-up archival copy of each user-loadable program and any update or revision. To the extent possible, End User will reproduce all confidentiality and proprietary notices on each of these copies. End User will not otherwise copy, translate, modify, adapt, decompile, disassemble, or reverse engineer the Licensed Programs.

4. Ownership

All Licensed Programs, copyrights, trademarks, trade names, trade secrets, and other proprietary rights in or related to the Licensed Programs are and will remain the exclusive property of VENDOR, whether or not registered under the laws of the Territory. End User will not contest VENDOR's proprietary rights or acquire any right in the Licensed Programs, except the limited use rights specified in the End-User Sublicense Agreement. VENDOR will own all rights in any copy, translation, modification, adaptation, or derivation of the Licensed Programs.

5. Confidentiality

End User acknowledges that the Licensed Programs incorporates confidential and proprietary information developed or acquired by VENDOR. End User will take all reasonable precautions necessary to safeguard the confidentiality of the Licensed Programs. End User will not allow the removal or defacement of any confidentiality or proprietary notice placed on items of the Licensed Programs.

6. Survival

The confidentiality obligations of End User will survive its expiration or termination of the End-User Sublicense Agreement for any reason.

7. Limitation of Liability

VENDOR WILL NOT BE LIABLE, IN CONTRACT, TORT, OR OTHERWISE, FOR ANY CONSEQUENTIAL, INDIRECT, SPECIAL, OR INCIDENTAL DAMAGE, INJURY, COST, OR EXPENSE, WHETHER FORESEEABLE OR UNFORESEEABLE (INCLUDING, BUT NOT LIMITED TO, PERSONAL INJURY, DEATH, PROPERTY DAMAGE, AND LOSS OF DATA, USE, OR PROFITS) WHICH MAY ARISE OUT OF OR IN CONNECTION WITH THIS AGREEMENT OR THE DELIVERY, USE, OR PERFORMANCE OF THE LICENSED PROGRAMS. IN NO EVENT WILL THE AGGREGATE LIABILITY WHICH VENDOR MAY INCUR IN ANY ACTION, WHETHER IN CONTRACT, TORT, OR OTHERWISE, EXCEED THE TOTAL AMOUNT ACTUALLY PAID TO VENDOR BY LICENSEE FOR THE SPECIFIC PRODUCT THAT DIRECTLY CAUSED THE DAMAGE.

8. Termination

Upon the expiration or termination of this End-User Sublicense Agreement, all rights granted to End User will immediately cease, and End User will promptly (i) purge the Licensed Programs from the CPU and all other computer systems, storage media, and other files; (ii) deliver to

LICENSEE or its designee the Licensed Programs and any other item within End User's possession or control that contains confidential information relating to the Licensed Programs; and (iii) deliver to LICENSEE with a notarized affidavit certifying that End User has complied with its termination obligations.

9. U.S. Export Restriction

End User acknowledges that the Licensed Programs may be subject to export restrictions imposed by the U.S. Government under the Export Administration Regulations. End User will (i) comply with all these restrictions; (ii) cooperate fully with VENDOR or LICENSEE in any official or unofficial audit or inspection relating to these restrictions; and (iii) not export or re-export, directly or indirectly, the Licensed Programs.

10. Assignment

End User acknowledges that if LICENSEE ceases to be VENDOR's authorized LICENSEE for any reason or otherwise at VENDOR's written request, LICENSEE's rights vis-à-vis End User under the End-User Sublicense Agreement will be automatically assigned to VENDOR or its designee. End User consents to this potential assignment and, at VENDOR's request, will execute any instrument which may be required to perfect the assignment.

11. Waiver, Amendment, Modification

LICENSEE and End User will not waive, amend or otherwise modify any provision of the End-User Sublicense Agreement that affects VENDOR's rights without the prior written approval of VENDOR.

12. Third-Party Beneficiary

End User recognizes that the provisions of the End-User Sublicense Agreement that govern the use, ownership, confidentiality, inspection, and re-exportation of the Licensed Programs, the termination and assignment of the Agreement and the limitation of liability are intended to inure to the benefit of VENDOR. End User acknowledges that (i) VENDOR has the right to enforce these provisions against End User, whether in its own name or the LICENSEE's name; (ii) VENDOR accepts this right; and (iii) LICENSEE confirms VENDOR's acceptance of this right by executing the End-User Sublicense Agreement.

EXHIBIT B
TO
INTERNATIONAL SOFTWARE MARKETING
AND LICENSE AGREEMENT

LIST OF LICENSED PROGRAMS AND TRADEMARKS

The "Licensed Programs" shall consist of:

Other trademarks:

EXHIBIT C
TO
INTERNATIONAL SOFTWARE MARKETING
AND LICENSE AGREEMENT

TERRITORY

The **"Territory"** shall consist of _____.

EXHIBIT D
TO
INTERNATIONAL SOFTWARE MARKETING
AND LICENSE AGREEMENT

REVENUE QUOTAS

For the purpose of this Agreement, the LICENSEE's **"Revenue Quotas"** shall be based on the total End-User Sublicense Fees derived by the Licensee in the Territory. Quota Year 1 shall begin on the Commencement Date and end on the following June 30. Each succeeding Quota Year shall begin on July 1.

Revenue Quotas—in U.S. $

Quota Year	Revenue Quota
Year 1	$
Year 2	$
Year 3 and thereafter:	150% of the prior year's Revenue Quota.

However, if LICENSEE fails to meet its Revenue Quota for the prior Quota Year and VENDOR does not elect to terminate this Agreement pursuant to Section 13 hereof, the Revenue Quota for the immediately subsequent Quota Year shall be agreed upon in writing by both parties. Revenue Quotas for the following years will again be one hundred fifty percent (150%) of the prior Quota Year's Revenue Quota. For purposes of calculating the Revenue Quotas, the U.S. dollar equivalent of the End-User Sublicense Fees shall be calculated at the official exchange rate quoted by *The Wall Street Journal* as of the date of the End-User Sublicense Agreement.

EXHIBIT E
TO
INTERNATIONAL SOFTWARE MARKETING
AND LICENSE AGREEMENT

EXISTING CUSTOMERS

EXHIBIT F
TO
INTERNATIONAL SOFTWARE MARKETING
AND LICENSE AGREEMENT

CONFIDENTIALITY AGREEMENT

To: VENDOR, Inc.

1. I, _____, understand that, as part of my duties as an employee of _____, (**"Company"**), I may have access to proprietary, confidential, and trade secret information of VENDOR, Inc. of Anytown, NY, USA (**"VENDOR"**), including, without limitation, certain data, designs, details, diagrams, inventions, know-how, programs, and techniques regarding VENDOR's computer software programs (**"Information"**). I acknowledge that all Information is proprietary, confidential, and trade secret information of VENDOR and that any unauthorized use or disclosure of any Information will result in significant damage to VENDOR.

2. In consideration for my continued employment at the Company, I agree to use all Information which I may receive or to which I may have access only for the performance of my employment obligations and

strictly in furtherance of the License Agreement and any other agreements entered into between VENDOR and the Company from time to time. I further agree to maintain the Information in strict confidence. I will not disclose the Information to any other person without the express written consent of VENDOR and will abide by the restrictions and terms regarding the use and protection of such Information as established by the Company and/or VENDOR from time to time.

3. Upon cessation of my employment with the Company, I will return all documents or media containing the Information to my supervisor. I agree that the above obligations regarding the maintenance of the Information in strict confidence and the restrictions on use or disclosure shall continue without any limitation after my employment with the Company has terminated, but shall cease to apply to any portion of the Information after it has come into the public domain without breach of contract or misfeasance by any person.

4. I further acknowledge that either the Company or VENDOR may enforce this Agreement against me and that my breach of this Agreement may result in my criminal prosecution.

In Witness Whereof, the undersigned has signed, sealed and delivered this Agreement as a deed on the date below written.

By: _____	Accepted By: _____
Name: _____	Name: _____
Title: _____	Title: _____
Date: _____	Date: _____

Appendix 4

International Travel Tips

Visas

U.S. citizens need visas to enter Argentina, Australia, Brazil, China, New Zealand, Saudi Arabia, and some other countries. They currently are not needed for casual business trips in Western Europe, Mexico, Japan, Singapore, or Hong Kong. Check with your travel agent to verify.

Airline Tickets

Nonrefundable "nonchangeable" tickets are almost always best for transoceanic travel. The return date or city can usually be changed for a nominal fee, and an unused ticket can always be used for credit against a future ticket on the same airline. The price is one-third to one-half of a full-fare coach. Within Europe, round-trip "excursion" fares on both airplanes and trains are often less expensive than regular one-way prices. Be sure to inquire, and be prepared to discard the return (although they are usually valid for one year).

Holidays and Weekends

Every day is a holiday somewhere in the world. Plan your trips around local holidays. Weekends in many Moslem countries are Thursday and Friday; in Israel they are Friday and Saturday.

Language

Obtain a pocket dictionary before you go, and learn a few phrases on the flight. "Hello, how are you," "I need a receipt, please," "Please bring me the check," and "Where is the bathroom?" often come in handy. Your foreign colleagues will appreciate any attempt you make at their language, no matter how clumsy. When speaking English to non-native speakers, concentrate on speaking slowly and clearly, and avoiding colloquialisms and idioms. It will be appreciated, and you are more likely to successfully complete your mission.

Changing Money

The best rate is obtained if you use your debit (not *credit*) card at an ATM. ATMs are widespread in Europe, and may be found elsewhere, too. Look to match a symbol on your card with one on the machine. Otherwise, changing at the airport or in a change shop is usually better than at the hotel. Travelers' checks usually get a better rate than cash (and are obviously safer). You can get foreign currency and foreign currency travelers' checks before you go from your bank, if you give a few days notice. There is no charge for changing a foreign currency traveler's check in that country.

Taxis

If there is not a meter, agree on a price before entering the taxi. If there is a meter, ask the driver to use it. If the price seems excessive upon arrival, get out of the taxi before disputing it with the driver. Sweden has many pirate taxis. French taxis are notorious—make sure you get your change, and that the driver does not consider it a "tip." Italian taxis can be (legally) exorbitant. Taxis from Milan's Malpensa Airport or Tokyo's Narita into the city are well over U.S. $100. There is good bus and train service from Narita. Do not expect to get a taxi receipt in Singapore, Hong Kong, or Latin America—they are just not available.

Tipping

A service charge is already added to most restaurant meals in Europe and Asia. The bill should tell you. In that case, no additional tip is expected, or just some small change may be given for excellent service. Most countries tip much less than the United States—about 10 percent would be normal for a meal. There is no tipping of anyone in Japan or China. Tipping taxi drivers in most countries is not expected. You can give bellpersons and porters the equivalent of U.S. $1 to $2 a bag, but it is not expected in Northern Europe.

Telephones

The number one rip-off is hotel telephone charges. Making an international call directly on your hotel phone can easily cost more than the price of the room. Be sure that you have a telephone credit card (AT&T, MCI, and Sprint work in most countries), and the list of local access numbers in each country. To order lists, call AT&T at +1-800-331-1140 extension 730, or Sprint at +1-800-877-4646. If you do not have a list, you can call AT&T in the United States collect from any country at +1-412-553-7458 extension 959 to obtain the local access number. These lists are updated frequently. It is also possible to order private local toll-free access numbers for both voice and data in many countries from Sprint or AT&T.

If you are unable to successfully reach these access numbers from your hotel room, the hotel operator can often connect you. The number of access lines is limited in some countries, and you may have to try repeatedly or during off hours. Note that you can call countries other than the United States from most foreign countries using a local access number and a telephone credit card (e.g., AT&T World Direct). Credit card calls can also be dialed from most public phones, but may require a coin to get a dial tone.

Be cautious and alert when speaking or keying your telephone credit card number at a public phone—it can easily be stolen. Kennedy Airport is notorious for this. Avoid if at all possible special "credit card phones" that take Visa, Mastercard, or American Express. These are extremely expensive. Telephone company credit card calls, though more reasonable than hotel-billed ones, are still expensive.

If you are calling the office or home, have your party call you back if the call will last for more than about three minutes. In almost all cases, calls originating in the United States are less expensive than the same calls originating abroad.

Security

Thieves abound—big cities are much alike (although Tokyo and Singapore are relatively safe). Rome and other Italian cities, Paris, and London are especially bad for property crime. Always keep a hand on your bags and cases while in public. Use hotel safes for valuables and passports.

Keep a credit card separate from your wallet, travelers' checks separate from cash, and records of travelers' check numbers separate from the checks. Keep a Xerox copy of the first page of your passport separate from your passport. Keep a list of your credit card account numbers separate from the cards, and at home. Safeguard airline tickets. Use inside pockets. If you are jostled, be especially alert. Innocent-looking children will happily pick your pockets in Italy.

Notebook Computers

A common scam at airport security works thus: one thief positions himself immediately in front of you in the queue. You put your computer on the x-ray belt. He takes a lot of time repeatedly going through the metal detector, removing watches, keys, coins, etc. Meanwhile, the other thief, already through security, casually picks up your computer and walks off with it, later discreetly exiting the secured area. Wait until you are next to go through the metal detector before you put your computer on the belt, and then watch it like a hawk.

Use the power-on password feature, as well as a disk password for removable hard disks. Never check computers as luggage. Keep file backups at home.

Carry phone adaptors if you intend to use a modem. Almost every foreign plug is different—RJ11 is not at all universal. Sometimes the hotel can lend you an adaptor, or has a business center with RJ11 access. With a small screwdriver you might be able to remove a cover plate on the phone or wall which will reveal a phone plug. The bathroom phone may unplug when the bedroom phone does not. Because computer dialing through a hotel PBX is not always possible, carry a 2-1 splitter and extra phone cable. That way you can dial through the telephone handset and then hang up, leaving the computer connected. Also, you will need power plug adaptors for recharging. These the hotel probably will have, or they can be purchased locally. Make sure that the charging transformer is compatible with the local voltage (frequently 220v).

Hotel Services

A concierge is found in most (not just fancy) international hotels. The concierge can reconfirm or change airline flights, assist you in arranging local transportation (bus and subway are cheaper and sometimes much faster than taxis), give you a free map of the city, and suggest and book restaurants. The hotel can often arrange a special shuttle to or from the airport. This is especially useful if you are arriving very late, or have a party with a lot of luggage. Check the prices of the minibar before you indulge. A $5 Coke is not uncommon. Hotel laundry is also usually very expensive. Sometimes you can find a regular laundry down the street that will do your clothes for one-third the price. Hair dryers often can be adjusted to run on 220v or can be borrowed from the hotel. Most hotels have 110v outlets for shavers only (these are low-current outlets, and will not run your hair dryer or recharge your computer).

Culture

Remember that people are usually proud of their own culture, country, and identity. Do not unfavorably compare to your own, but look for ways to expand your own appreciation of diversity.

Toasts

Language	Toast	Pronounce
English	cheers	cheers
Japanese	kampai	calm'-pie'
German	prost	proast
French	sante	san-tay
Spanish	salud	sah-lood'
Italian	cin cin	chin chin
Chinese	gam bei	gom bay

For a more complete list of toasts, see Roger E. Axtell's *Do's and Taboos of Hosting International Visitors*.

Appendix 5

Internet Resource Guide

A GUIDE TO INTERNATIONAL TRADE
RESOURCES ON THE INTERNET

Trade Information Center
Office of Export Promotion Coordination, Trade Development
(800) USA-TRAD(E)
April 12, 1996

Fourth Edition

Please be aware that this is *NOT* a comprehensive guide of all of the international trade resources on the Internet. This list does not represent an endorsement of any particular service, product, or information source by the U.S. Department of Commerce or the International Trade Administration. Some of the resources listed are private, commercial sites and may charge a fee for access to their services. Inclusion of sources on this list is at the discretion of the Trade Information Center and is subject to change without notice.

[Note: The information that follows has been adapted from the original U.S. Department of Commerce publication for inclusion in this book.]

The following designations will help you determine the type of information that can be found at the web sites listed here:

1 = Comprehensive sources of international trade information
2 = Region-specific information
3 = Industry-specific information
4 = Trade contacts and leads
5 = International trade services
6 = Government resources for export promotion
7 = International trade law

American Chamber of Commerce in Brazil
http://www.amcham.com.br
- Regional information (Brazil)   2

American National Standards Institute (ANSI)
http://www.ansi.org/home.html
- Information on U.S. standards   5, 6

AmericasNet at Florida State University
http://americas.fiu.edu/index.html
- America's trade forum   2

ANANSE International Trade Law Project
http://itl.irv.uit.no/trade_law/
- International organizations and conventions   7

A.R. Vogue Corporation
http://www.bekkoame.or.jp/~tomatell/business/vogue.htm
- Trade leads and trade catalogues   4

Asia Development Bank
http://www.asiandevbank.org/
- ADB information, finance   5

Asia in Cyberspace
http://silkroute.com/silkroute/asia/rsrc/country/index.html
- Asian country information   2

Asian Trade Links
http://adam.com.au/~atl-aust
- Australian firm with Asian contacts   2, 5

Assist International
http://www.assist-intl.com
- Comprehensive export information   1

Atlanta International Magazine
http://www.aimlink.com/at/mag
- Regional information (Southeast United States)   2, 4

Australian Embassy
http://www.aust.emb.nw.dc.us/intrade.htm
- Regional information (Australia and Asia)   2

Big Dreams
http://www.wimsey.com/~duncans
- Information on starting a business   1

BizPro
http://www.bizpro.com
- Business listings on the Web   4, 5

BizWeb
http://www.bizweb.com
- Index of commerical Web sites   5

Bureau of National Affairs
http://www.bna.com
- Legislative and regulatory information, publications   5, 7

Business Link
http://www.jsp.fi/
- Finnish trading company (Russia)   2, 5

Business Publications
gopher://gopher.enews.com:70/11/magazines/category/business/
international
- Business publications   1

Commercial News Services
http://www.jou.ufl.edu/comres/webjou.htm.
- Newspapers on-line   5

Congressional Record for 104th Congress
http://thomas.loc.gov/
- Congressional documents   7

Consolidated Freightways
http://www.cnf.com/
- Transportation information   5

Costa Rica Web Server
http://ns.cr/ecconeg.html
- Links to sites in Costa Rica   2

Daily International News
http://www.helsinki.fi/~lsaarine/news.html
- Business and economic news   1

Dharani Export Import Services, Ltd.
http://www.webindia.com/cust/india/dharani/dharani.html
- Indian trading company   2

Dun & Bradstreet
http://www.dbisna.com/
- Information services   1, 5

Electronic Embassy
http://www.embassy.org
- Foreign embassies in District of Columbia   1, 2

Elvis Server
http://www.elvis.msk.su
- Moscow service provider; Russian links   2

Eniitco General Trading Europe, AB
http://www.pi.se/eniitco/index.html
- Swedish trading company   2

Entrepreneurs
http://sashimi.wwa.com/~notime/eotw/EOTW.html
- Business information for entrepreneurs   1

Export Leads
LP.Export@mailback.com
  • Bulletin board system (BBS) for export leads 4

Export Legal Assistance Network (ELAN)
http://web.miep.org/elan
  • Legal assistance 7

Export Price Indices and Percent Change
gopher://una.hh.lib.umich.edu/0/ebb/price/exim-4.bis
  • Pricing information 5

Export Today Magazine
http://www.exporttoday.com
  • Export Today Magazine 1, 5

Export USA
http://www.exportusa.com
  • Executive resource for comprehensive information 1

Far East Business Directory
http://www.net-trade.com
  • Regional information on the Far East 2

FedWorld
http://www.fedworld.gov/
  • Information locator for U.S. Government 1

Federal Government WWW Servers
http://www.fie.com/
  • Springboard to most Federal home pages 1

Federation of International Trade Associations
http://www.webhead.com/FITA/home.html
  • Organizations of trade associations (with links) 5

FINWeb
http://www.finweb.com/
  • Finance and economic information 1, 5

Fletcher School of Law & Diplomacy
http://www.tufts.edu/fletcher/multilaterals.html
  • Multilateral conventions 7

Global Ukraine
http://www.gu.kiev.ua/
- Information on Ukraine and Kiev 2

Glossary of International Trade Terms
http://circleintl.com
- Trade terms 2, 5

GoldSite Europe
http://www.gold.net:80/
- Information and links to Europe 2

Graduate Institute of International Studies
http://heiwww.unige.ch/gatt/final_act
- GATT agreement (final text) 7

Guide to Marketing on the Internet
http://www.industry.net/guide.html
- Marketing guide 5

Holt's Stock Market Reports
http://metro.turnpike.net/holt/index.html
- Information on international financial markets 2

IBEX Exchange
http://www.ibex.com/
- Listing of exporting companies 1, 4

IBEX Yellow Pages
http://www.cba.uh.edu/ylowpges/yi.html
- Listing of exporting companies 1, 4, 5

IMEX Exchange
http://www.imex.com/
- Trade leads, general information 1, 4

Impex Connect
http://www.aztec.co.za/impex
- South African trading company 2

Import/Export Connection
http://www.cam.org/~sailor/imexcon.htm/
- Trade leads 4

International Trade Organizations
http://www.yahoo.com/Economy/Organizations/International_Trade/
- Search engine   5

International Trade Resources
http://www.infomanage.com/international/trade
- Trade resource links   1

Internet Group
http://www.tig.com
- Internet marketing group   5

Internet Guide to Japan
http://fuji.stanford.edu/japan_information_guide.html
- Information about Japan   2

Internet Tradeline
http://www.intrade.com/
- General information, trade leads   4, 5

Intertrade Mercantile Exchange
http://www.intergroup.com/mercantile
- Trading forum   4, 5

Japan Computer Science Co., Ltd.
http://www.jcsnet.or.jp/v-city/trade/guide-e/index-e.html
- Japanese market   2

Japan External Trade Organization (JETRO)
http://www.jetro.go.jp
- Regional information (Japan)   2

Japan-MITI
http://glocom.ac.jp/NEWS/MITI
- MITI's program for information infrastructure   2

Japanese Ministry of International Trade and Industry
http://www.miti.go.jp
- Regional information (Japan)   2

J.J.L. Associates
http://www.cityscape.co.uk/users/dr39/
- Customs and freight (Europe)   2, 5

KEYMEXX
http://jsasoc.com/keymexx.html
- Regional information (Mexico)   2

Knowledge Web
http://www.kweb.com
- Trade show listings   5

Koblas Currency Converter
http://gnn.com/cgi-bin/gnn/currency
- Exchange rates for about 50 countires   . 2

KoreaWeb Information Services
http://www.webcom.com/~koreaweb
- Links to sites in South Korea   2

Latin American Trade Council of Oregon
http://www.teleport.com/~tmiles/latco.htm/
- Regional information (Oregon, Latin America)   2

Latin American Trade and Information Network
http://www.latinet.com
- Latin American trade information   2, 4

Latin American/Caribbean Bulletin
http://www.ita.doc.gov/region/latinam/
- LAC business bulletin   2

LatinoWeb Business
http://www.latinoweb.com/favision/business.htm
- Trade leads; regional information (Latin America)   2, 4

Library of Commerce
http://www.loc.gov/
- Information and research   1

Mariner Systems, Inc.
http://msi.marsys.com/
- Shipping rates, schedules, tarrifs, etc.   5

Market Link
http://m-link.com
- Multilingual directories and resources   1

Ministry of International Trade and Industry (MITI)
http://www.miti.go.jp/
- Regional information (Japan)   2

NAFTA
gopher://umslvma.umsl.edu:70/11/library/govdocs/naftaf
- Text of agreement   2, 7

NAFTAnet Small Business Information
http://www.naftanet/smallbiz.htm
- NAFTA   2, 5

National Technical Information Service
http://www.fedworld.gov/ntis/business/ibus.htm
- Government international trade publications   1

National Trade Data Bank
http://www.stat-usa.gov
- Market information and research   1

Netherlands Contacts
http://www.euronet.nl/users/gandy/index.html
- Information on the Netherlands   2

New York Library System
http://www.nysernet.org/
- Information and research   1

New York Times, The
http://www.nytimefax.com
- *The New York Times* newspaper   1

Nippon Telephone and Telegraph (NTT)
http://www.ntt.jp
- Regional information (Japan)   2

North Carolina International Trade Notes
http://www.ces.ncsu.edu/itd/catalog.html
- Trade information and leads   1, 2, 4

Notices of Foreign Govenment Standards
gopher://gopher.counterpoint.com:
2003/11/Foreign%20Government%20Standards   5, 7

Online Manufacturers Network
http://www.mfrnet.com
- Advertising/marketing   5

Open Markets Commercial Sites
http://www.directory.net/
- U.S. suppliers   4

Organization of American States
http://www.sice.oas.org
- Regional information (Latin America)   2

PangaeaNet Home Page
http://www.pangaea.net/homepage.htm
- BBS trade leads and marketing information   1, 4

Pennsylvania International BusinessNet
http://www.pitt.edu/~wpaintl/
- Market information, export assistance,
  regional information (PA)   1, 2, 5

Poppe Tyson Advertising and Public Relations
http://www.poppe.com:8400
- Marketing and online services   5

ProTRADE Forum
http://www.cityscape.co.uk/users/bm22/pt.html
- Information on Compuserve's ProTRADE forum   1

Romanian Home Page (Burhala)
http://werple.apana.org.au/~florin/default.html
- Romanian information   2

Russian Trade Connection
http://www.lh.com/rtc/
- Russian information   2

Simon Fraser's David See-Chai Lan
Centre International Commission
http://hoshi.cic.sfu.ca/11/dlam/business/forum
  • Regional information (Japan)   2

Small Business Administration (SBA)
http://www.sbaonline.sba.gov
  • Information including finance for small exporter   1, 5, 6

Small Business Foundation of America
http://web.miep.org/sbfa/
  • Information on starting a business   1

Somers & Associates
http://ppp.jax-inter.net/ispy/
  • Business intelligence and investigation   5

Starting Point
http://www.stpt.com/
  • International and business news   1, 4

Stat-USA
http://www.stat-usa.gov
  • National Trade Data Bank and Export Bulletin Board   1

State Export Statistics
http://www.ita.doc.gov/industry/otea/state
  • State-by-state export stats   2, 5, 6

Taiwan Internet Gateway
http://pristine.com.tw/
  • Multilingual links to Taiwan and Asia   2

Taiwan WWW Sites
http://peacock.tnjc.edu.tw/organ.html
  • Links to sites in Taiwan   2

Texas-One Home Page (TX DOC)
http://www.texas-one.org
  • Regional information (United States)   2

TradePort
http://tradeport.org/
- Comprehensive information for California exporters   1, 5

Traders' Connection
http://www.trader.com
- Member-based service; advertising   5

Trade Scope
http://www.tradescope.com/
- Insurance, credit reports   1, 4, 5

Tradescope Home Page
http://www.tradescope.com/
- Trade leads, marketing information   1, 4

Trade Show Central
http://www.tscentral.com
- Trade show listings   5

Trade Trading (Taiwan)
http://trace.com.tw
- Taiwanese trading company/Asian links   2

Trade Zone
http://www.tradezone.com/tz/trdzone.html
- Global trade information/mail order how-to   1, 6

UNCTAD Gopher
gopher://unicc.org/1/ITC
- United Nations Conference on Trade and Development; extensive stats and trade information   1, 5

Uniform Commerical Code (Cornell University)
http://www.law.cornell.edu/ucc/ucc.table.html
- Uniform Commercial Code   7

UNISPHERE
http://www.nando.net/uni/
- High-tech industries   3

USDA Foreign Agricultural Service
http://www.usda.gov:/8000/fas//
- Agricultural export information 6

U.S. Department of State
http://www.stolaf.edu/network/travel-advisories.html
- Political and economic climates around the world 2, 6

USDOC (U.S. Department of Commerce)
http://www.doc.gov/
- Home page for DOC 1, 5, 6

USDOC Big Emerging Markets
http://www.stat-usa.gov/itabems.html
- Regional information (BEMs) 2, 6

USDOC Bureau of Export Administration (BXA)
http://www.doc.gov/resources/BXA_infor.html
- Information on BXA function and contacts 5, 6

USDOC Global Export Market Information System
http://www.itaiep.doc.gov/
- BEMs, Eastern Europe Business Information Center (EEBIC), Business Information Service for the Newly Independent States (BISNIS), NAFTA 2, 6

USDOC Import Administration
http://www.ita.doc.gov/import_admin/records/
- U.S. import restrictions and regulations 2, 6

USDOC International Trade Administration
http://www.ita.doc.gov/
- General information, comprehensive 2, 6

USDOC Japan Export Information Center
http://www.ita.doc.gov/regional/geo_region/japan
- Regional information (Japan) 2, 6

U.S. Government Printing Office
http://www.access.gpo.gov/
- Directory of government documents 6

World Bank
http://www.worldbank.org/
- World Bank information, finance 5

World Bank International Trade Division
http://www.worldbank.org/html/iecit/iecit.html
- World Bank information on trade 1

World Bank, Risk Trends in Developing Countries
http://quasar.poly.edu:9090/WorldBank/tde-home.html
- Information on less developed countries (LDCs) 2

World Business Exchange
http://www.wbenet.com/
- Information on exporting 1

World Currency Converter
http://www.dna.lth.se/cgi-bin/kurt/rates
- Converts most world currencies 5

World Wide Trade
http://www.nas.com/~westg/
- Ads, business opportunities, consumer products 1, 5

WWW Servers for Former Soviet Union
http://www.w3.org/hypertext/DataSources/bySubject/Overview.html
- Links to all known sites in former USSR 2

WWW Servers in Sweden
http://www.sunet.se/sweden
- Links to Swedish sites 2

Wyvern Business Library
http://www.cityscape.co.uk
- Business books 1

Yahoo
http://www.yahoo.com/
- Search engine 5

Appendix 6

Checklist When Writing
for an International Audience

Most articles and newsletters written for U.S. readers can, with minimal modification, be made suitable for an international English readership. Following are some guidelines:

addresses: Zip code is an American term for the general term, postal code. The postal code appears before the city in most countries. Include the country name in all addresses, United States or foreign. Appendix V of *Developing International Software* by Nadine Kano is an excellent reference to the preferred forms of addresses in most countries.

collective words: Avoid words like "countrywide" or "national" unless the country involved is specified. Statistics should also be qualified as necessary (e.g., there are 2,000 users of the product—United States? worldwide?).

currency: Hong Kong, Canada, Australia, New Zealand, the United States, Singapore, the Bahamas, and others all use dollars. If there is any likelihood of confusion, identify as U.S. $100, AUD 24.000, etc. Billion means million million in most other English-speaking countries. To be clear, use thousand million.

dates: The international format is day/month/year. To avoid confusion spell the month, e.g., 29 August, 1997.

globes: Pictures of the globe showing only the western hemisphere (the common kind in the United States) are insensitive to readers from the other half of the world. Instead, use a "peeled orange," or "squashed oval" style world map, which shows all continents.

measures: Most of the world uses the metric system. Measures like inches, feet, yards, miles, gallons, quarts, and acres are confusing to metric readers. Use both, e.g., ten miles (16.2 km).

paper size: The U.S. "standard" 8 1/2 x 11 is a bit shorter and wider than the worldwide metric standard A4.

postage: Preprinted postage and return mailers generally will not work from abroad. Alternatives should be provided.

reader response: Company phone numbers and address should be arranged so that they can be conveniently stickered over by VARs or distributors wanting to use the same piece in their territories.

seasons: Northern Hemisphere summer is Southern Hemisphere winter. Avoid these terms as they are meaningless on a global basis. Use months or calendar quarters instead.

telephone and fax numbers: The country code for the United States is 1. All U.S. telephone and fax numbers should begin with +1, for example: +1-602-555-0050. The "+" denotes the international access code particular to the caller's country. 1-800 and 1-888 toll-free numbers generally do not work from abroad; always accompany them with the toll number alternative.

temperature: Most of the world uses centigrade, not Fahrenheit. Be sure to clarify what kind of degrees you mean or, better yet, use both.

times: Most countries use the twenty-four-hour system, e.g., 15:30 is 3:30pm. However, the latter will be understood.

Bibliography

Acuff, Frank L. *How to Negotiate Anything with Anyone Anywhere Around the World.* New York: American Management Association, 1992.

Ambrosio, Joanna. Should You Export That Software? *Computerworld,* 2 August 1993: p. 75.

Anonymous. Exporting Pays Off. *Business America,* October 1994: p. 32. (Success story of Folio Corp. software firm.)

Axtell, Roger E. *Do's and Taboos Around the World.* New York: John Wiley and Sons, 1990.

Axtell, Roger E. *Do's and Taboos of Hosting International Visitors.* New York: John Wiley and Sons, 1990.

Clapes, Anthony Lawrence. *Softwars: The Legal Battles for Control of the Global Software Industry.* Westport, CT: Quorum Books, 1993.

Fath, William. *How to Develop and Manage Successful Distributor Channels in World Markets.* New York: Amacom, 1995.

Graham, John L., and Yoshihiro Sano. *Smart Bargaining: Doing Business with the Japanese.* Cambridge, MA: Ballinger Publishing Company, 1984.

Griffin, Trenholme J., and W. Russell Daggett. *The Global Negotiator.* Delran, NJ: Harper Business, 1990.

Hall, Edward T. *Understanding Cultural Differences.* Yarmouth, ME: Intercultural Press, 1990.

Heichler, Elizabeth. When GUIs and Cultures Collide. *Computerworld,* 25 September 1995.

Henderson, Carter. U.S. Small Business Heads Overseas. *In Business,* November/December, 1995.

Kane, George. Sales Management Strategies for Asia. *Software Developer & Publisher,* September/October, 1996: p. 41.

Kano, Nadine. *Developing International Software*: A Handbook for International Software Design. Redmond, WA: Microsoft Press, 1995.

Kato, Hiroki, and Joan Kato. *Understanding and Working with the Japanese Business World.* Englewood Cliffs, NJ: Prentice-Hall, 1992.

Levitt, Theodore. *The Marketing Imagination.* New York: Free Press, 1986.

Ludolph, Charles. Winds of Change: Europe and Virginia in the 21st Century. Virginia Conference on World Trade, Williamsburg, VA, October 21, 1996.

Maggiori, Herman J. *How to Make the World Your Market: The International Sales and Marketing Handbook.* Mission Hills, CA: Burning Gate Press, 1992.

Moore, Geoffrey A. *Crossing the Chasm.* New York: Harper Business, 1991.

Morris-Lee, James. The Internet: Marketers Deal with Buyer Perceptions Through Better Security. *Direct Marketing,* January 1996: pp. 38-40.

Nadel, Jack. *Cracking the Global Market: How to Do Business Around the Corner and Around the World.* New York: American Management Association, 1987.

Norment & Associates, Inc. *Outlook for the European Software Market.* Arlington, VA: Information Technology Association of America, 1993.

Ouchi, William G. *Theory Z.* Reading, MA: Addison-Wesley, 1981.

Platt, Polly. Foreign Exchanges. *U.S. Air Magazine,* February 1996.

Rowlan, Diana. *Japanese Business Etiquette—A Practical Guide to Success with the Japanese.* New York: Warner Books, 1993.

Royal, Weld F. Passport to Peril? *Sales & Marketing Management,* December 1994.

Schenot, Robert. *How to Sell Your Software.* New York: J. Wiley, 1994.

Zimmerman, Mark. *How to Do Business with the Japanese.* New York: Random House, 1985.

Other Publications

Directory of International Research Firms. Published by *Marketing News*, Chicago, IL, 1995.

Entrepreneur. 1995 Corruption Index, February 1996.

The European Information Marketplace: Technology, Infrastructure and Services. Office of Service Industries, U.S. Department of Commerce, Washington, DC, 1996.

Information Services Industry in Japan. Published by the Japan Information Service Industry Association, Tokyo, 1995.

International Do's and Don'ts of the PC Software Industry. Arlington, VA: Software Publishers' Association, 1993.

"The International News Flash." Virginia Department of Economic Development, Division of International Trade and Investment, Richmond, VA, June 1996.

Martindale-Hubbell Law Directory. New Providence, NJ: Martindale-Hubbell, 1996.

Selling Software in the Global Market, 1996-97. Alpharetta, GA: Culpepper and Associates, 1996.

Serving the European Union: A Citizen's Guide to the Institutions of the European Union. Office of Official Publications of the European Communities, Luxembourg, 1995.

The Single Market. Office of Official Publications of the European Communities, Luxembourg, 1995.

Worldwide Information Technology Market. International Data Corporation, Framingham, MA, 1996.

Index

Page numbers followed by the letter "t" indicate tables; those followed by the letter "f" indicate figures.

Order Your Own Copy of
This Important Book for Your Personal Library!

GUIDE TO SOFTWARE EXPORT
A Handbook for International Software Sales

_____ in hardbound at $49.95 (ISBN: 0-7890-0143-8)

COST OF BOOKS_____	☐ **BILL ME LATER:** ($5 service charge will be added) (Bill-me option is good on US/Canada/Mexico orders only; not good to jobbers, wholesalers, or subscription agencies.)
OUTSIDE USA/CANADA/ MEXICO: ADD 20%_____	
POSTAGE & HANDLING_____ (US: $3.00 for first book & $1.25 for each additional book) Outside US: $4.75 for first book & $1.75 for each additional book)	☐ Check here if billing address is different from shipping address and attach purchase order and billing address information. Signature_____
SUBTOTAL_____	☐ **PAYMENT ENCLOSED: $**_____
IN CANADA: ADD 7% GST _____	☐ **PLEASE CHARGE TO MY CREDIT CARD.**
STATE TAX_____ (NY, OH & MN residents, please add appropriate local sales tax)	☐ Visa ☐ MasterCard ☐ AmEx ☐ Discover ☐ Diner's Club
FINAL TOTAL_____ (If paying in Canadian funds, convert using the current exchange rate. UNESCO coupons welcome.)	Account # _____ Exp. Date _____ Signature _____

Prices in US dollars and subject to change without notice.

NAME _____

INSTITUTION _____

ADDRESS _____

CITY _____

STATE/ZIP _____

COUNTRY _____ COUNTY (NY residents only) _____

TEL _____ FAX _____

E-MAIL_____

May we use your e-mail address for confirmations and other types of information? ☐ Yes ☐ No

Order From Your Local Bookstore or Directly From
The Haworth Press, Inc.
10 Alice Street, Binghamton, New York 13904-1580 • USA
TELEPHONE: 1-800-HAWORTH (1-800-429-6784) / Outside US/Canada: (607) 722-5857
FAX: 1-800-895-0582 / Outside US/Canada: (607) 772-6362
E-mail: getinfo@haworth.com
PLEASE PHOTOCOPY THIS FORM FOR YOUR PERSONAL USE.

BOF96